I0153199

LIVE LIGHT ABOVE THE NEGATIVITY

REFLECTIONS AND DEVOTIONALS FOR PERSONAL GROWTH FOR CHRISTIAN LIVING

TREVOR H LUND

IMAGINE PUBLISHING - A DIVISION OF LIVE LIGHT

PUBLICATIONS

© 2022 Trevor H Lund

All Rights Reserved. No part of this publication may be reproduced, stored in a retrieval system, or transmitted, in any form or in any means – by electronic, mechanical, photocopying, recording or otherwise – without prior written permission.

ISBN – Hardcover – 978-1-897409-32-9

ISBN - Print - 978-1-897409-29-9

ISBN - ebook - 978-1-897409-30-5

ISBN - Large Print - 978-1-897409-31-2

Published through Imagine Publishing 3428 – 99 Street Suite 444, Edmonton, Alberta, Canada, T6E 5X5

Cover Photo by Janko Ferlic:
https://www.pexels.com/photo/trees-and-grass-field-603189/

CONTENTS

WHAT PEOPLE HAVE SAID

Our lives move at such a fast pace that we don't fully see the poor habits that have become part of us. The Fast from Negativity will provide you with the tools you need to set healthy, positive patterns in your life.

- Kevin Fricker

The church needs to wake up! Trevor has done a magnificent job challenging every believer to be a positive believer.

- Wynne Lewis

It's good to see us being challenged to sincerely look at how we think, speak and live as Christians. Trevor touches on the "nitty-gritty" issues of how to develop our character to be more in line with what the Word of God says.

- Rodney Francis

From people who have fasted from negativity:

"While I was fasting from negativity, my supervisor gave me a gift certificate for $100 for being the most positive person in the company."
(your results may vary)

"After the negativity fast my boss asked what my secret was for looking younger as I got older. I had to mention giving up negativity."
(your results may vary)

KEY CONCEPTS

So you have taken up a challenge that's too big not to die for, now what?

That's not meant to turn you back from the starting line, but it is to get you to count the costs before you begin. If you're feeling a little trepidation, that's OK. Read through this chapter and the next, but as you do, keep a couple of key thoughts in your mind.

First, God is more concerned about your character than your comfort. His goal is to conform you into the likeness of His son (Romans 8:29). Yes, He loves you the way you are, but He loves you too much to let you stay that way. You have too many people to impact for His Kingdom that you can't influence until more of Christ is seen in you.

I'm not writing to brand-new followers of Christ here. It's not just the newly planted that needs deeper roots. Even if you're a tree planted by the river of God whose leaves produce fruit in their season, your roots need to continue to reach towards the rich nutrients the river brings. Your branches need to continue to stretch towards the life-giving sun.

A tree grows towards the light, but it will never reach the sun. We're all on a journey, and we'll never be able to say, "I've arrived." Nebuchadnezzar said that while on a roof in Babylon, and look at what happened the next seven years of his life.

So remember, all of us can become more like Christ—that's the great adventure we're on.

Second, as you read these introductory chapters, realize you can do all things through Christ who strengthens you. The work that He's begun in you, He'll be faithful to complete. He empowers you to accomplish every good work prompted by faith. God doesn't give you a test, so you can fail. Even though negativity is one of the toughest things you can fast from, you can do it! The same power that raised Jesus from the dead is alive within you (Ephesians 1:17-20).

With these thoughts in mind, let's examine some questions around a fast from negativity.

What is a Negativity Fast?

A "fast" is abstaining from something—usually food—for spiritual reasons, for a reason and set period.

Daniel fasted from wine, meat and choice foods for 21 days when he was awaiting an answer from God. Jesus fasted from food for 40 days at the start of His ministry.

Isaiah 58 lays out the fast that is acceptable to God and the blessing that comes from that kind of fast.

> 'We have fasted before you!' they say. 'Why aren't you impressed? We have been very hard on ourselves, and you don't even notice it!' "I will tell you why!" I respond. "It's because you are fasting to please yourselves. Even while you fast, you keep oppressing your workers. What good is fasting when you keep on fighting and quarreling? This kind of fasting will never get you anywhere with me. You humble yourselves by going through the motions of penance, bowing your heads like reeds bending in the wind. You dress in burlap and cover yourselves with ashes. Is this what you call fasting? Do you really think this will please the Lord? "No, this is the kind of fasting I want: Free those who are wrongly imprisoned; lighten the burden of those who work for you. Let the oppressed go free, and remove the chains that bind people. Share your food with the hungry, and give shelter to the homeless. Give clothes to those who need them, and do not hide from relatives who need your

> help. "Then your salvation will come like the dawn, and your wounds will quickly heal. Your godliness will lead you forward, and the glory of the Lord will protect you from behind. Then, when you call, the Lord will answer. 'Yes, I am here,' he will quickly reply. "Remove the heavy yoke of oppression. Stop pointing your finger and spreading vicious rumors! Feed the hungry, and help those in trouble. Then your light will shine out from the darkness, and the darkness around you will be as bright as noon. The Lord will guide you continually, giving you water when you are dry and restoring your strength. You will be like a well-watered garden, like an ever-flowing spring. Some of you will rebuild the deserted ruins of your cities. Then you will be known as a rebuilder of walls and a restorer of homes. "Keep the Sabbath day holy. Don't pursue your own interests on that day, but enjoy the Sabbath and speak of it with delight as the Lord's holy day. Honor the Sabbath in everything you do on that day, and don't follow your own desires or talk idly. Then the Lord will be your delight. I will give you great honor and satisfy you with the inheritance I promised to your ancestor Jacob. I, the Lord, have spoken!" (NLT)

This is how we fast when we fast from negativity.

We've defined "negativity," as "any thought, word, or action that is contrary to the will of God expressed in Scripture."

Bill Johnson, pastor of Bethel Church in Redding, California, says:

> "I cannot afford to have any thought in my head that's not His."

This applies to all of us. Thoughts lead to words and actions, so the main battlefield when we fast from negativity will be our minds.

We fast from negativity because we want our thoughts, words, and actions to reflect the goodness and greatness of God.

Why should I fast from negativity?

Some individuals correctly point out that our thoughts, words, and actions should always reflect God's goodness and greatness. We are followers of Christ, after all.

I prefer to think of the fast approach as an offer of amnesty. The police in Canada will often hold a turn-in-your-illegal-weapons-without-being-charged campaign to get unregistered weapons away from the potential of theft.

A fast gives followers of Christ the opportunity to act more like Christ without the condemnation that they haven't been consistently acting like Christ.

Second, having positive thoughts, words, and actions for 46 days gives us a great opportunity to shape our character. Fasting from negativity should get you to the place where not being negative becomes a natural part of your life. Tricking yourself into starting is a great way to get any goal accomplished.

When should I fast from negativity?

I often do negativity fasts over Lent. That's why the reflections and devotionals now are 46 days. Don't wait until you feel like abstaining from any thought, word, or action that is contrary to the will of God expressed in Scripture. It's a decision you need to make ahead of time.

Don't set your alarm for 5 AM and leave the decision if you'll get up when the alarm goes off to when the alarm goes off. Your intention of spending time alone with God will never amount to action until you make the decision ahead of time to make the time.

There will be ample times when conditions will be conducive for you to choose to be negative over the next 46 days. Your decision to fast from negativity, the power of the Holy Spirit, and knowledge that with every temptation God provides a way out of that temptation, will be what stops you from choosing to be negative when conditions are conducive.

If you're putting off bringing every thought captive and making obedient to Christ, you need to consider something very carefully. Can you tell God when and how you'll be obedient to Him?

Saul tried to keep the best of the Amalekite animals, saying they would be a sacrifice to God. But he disobeyed God's command to completely destroy this people whose sin reached its full measure. Samuel's response was:

> *"What is more pleasing to the Lord: your burnt offerings and sacrifices or your obedience to his voice? Listen! Obedience is better than sacrifice, and submission is better than offering the fat of rams. Rebellion is as sinful as witchcraft, and stubbornness as bad as worshiping idols. So because you have rejected the command of the Lord, he has rejected you as king."* 1 Samuel 15:22-23 (NLT)

Don't make excuses to allow negativity to remain in your life.

What to Expect

Congratulations on choosing to abstain from every thought word and action that is not in line with the will of God expressed in Scripture. It's not an easy challenge, but the Holy Spirit will help you because He wants to conform you more and more into the image of Christ.

I want to help as well. Since 2006 I've been helping Christians to fast from negativity to help live life more positively.

Every day you have a reflection and a devotional. The reflection is scripture that has been personalized with a question we can ask ourselves or Holy Spirit how we are currently aligning with it.

The Devotional has the following format...

Reflection

Personalized Bible verses to help examine our thoughts and actions.

Scripture

Scripture reading for the day

Thought

A thought from the Scripture

Prayer

A prayer based on the thought

Challenge

A challenge for the day to help you live out the thought

Declaration

An agreement with God's will expressed in Scripture that you can speak over yourself or the situation.

As you progress through each section, you'll move from negativity to positivity. The Steps include: How to fast From negativity, Be prepared for your enemy, Let fruit be fruit, The Real me, Forgiveness is key, Live unoffended at God, Strengthen yourself in the Lord, and finally Change your everyday world.

It also helps to put an elastic around your wrist that you can snap every time you have a word, thought, or action that is negative. A little behaviour modification never really hurt anyone...although the elastic might if your family members pull it for you.

A negativity fast is a challenge too big not to die for, but the rewards far outweigh the risks. Can you imagine life with less worry or fear? Can you think what it would be like to have no fear of bad news when it comes? What would it be like to feel God's presence with you at all times?

Amazing things happen when we choose to agree with God's thoughts for us. This happens as we fast from negativity.

It's going to be a fun adventure. I'm here for you along the way. Email me your questions and laments at revtrev@livelight.ca or connect with me at https://TrevorLund.com. I'm happy to help and pray for you along the way.

It's going to be awesome!

FROM THE AUTHOR

I so enjoy seeing what God is doing in the hearts and lives of people.

I'm here to tell you that you can live life above the negativity. It doesn't matter what your circumstances are. It doesn't matter what your bank account says. The phone call that drops you to your knees doesn't matter. It doesn't matter what your work is like. It may matter what your home is like, but we'll work on that over 46 days. What matters is:

- You are a child of the King(Matthew 6:9-10).
- You are a friend of God (John 15:15).
- You have the Spirit of wisdom and counsel to help you (Isaiah 11:1-3).
- You have the Kingdom of God around you and growing within you (Luke 17:21).
- You have the same power that raised Christ Jesus from the dead alive in you (Ephesians 1:19-20).

The number of people who have gone through a negativity fast with me has blown me away. Churches in Canada, the US, England and Australia and has contacted me each of them participate as they want.

It has amazed me how it's developed.

- A vicar in England created a small group study based on the material.
- A youth leader in the US developed a youth curriculum.
- There are groups on Facebook that meet to encourage people to live positively.

When I started, there was not one Christian site on the first 30 pages of Google that taught on negativity fasts. I remember checking once and we were #1 and ranked higher than Oprah on Google for a negativity fast... and she was promoting in on her show. We really exploded then.

A negativity fast is an opportunity to change our thoughts, our words and our actions so they agree with God's. It's a chance for us to train ourselves to be intentional with what we think, what we say, and what we do. It is not about following a legalistic list of rules. It is about experiencing and responding to the grace of God in our lives.

There are three truths I need to agree with so I can Live LIGHT Above the negativity.

1. Negativity is any thought, word, or action that is not in agreement with the will of God expressed in the Bible.

2. I can't control other people's thoughts, words, or actions. I can only control mine - with Holy Spirit's help.

3. Bringing my thoughts, words and actions more into agreement with the will of God expressed in the Bible —with Holy Spirit's help—can change the atmosphere in my everyday world, no matter how negative it is.

Word Association

I'd like to do a little word association game with you to make sure that we're all on the same page.

You plant a kernel of corn and you expect...corn will grow.

You plant a wheat seed and you expect...wheat.

You plant an acorn and you expect...an oak tree.

Like produces like, right? On the third day God said, "Let there be vegetation and let their seeds reproduce after their own kind." (Genesis 1:11-12) He's ordained that what we sow we reap. Right?

I know this might seem a little basic, but you can tell it's going somewhere, right?

When you see a lemon squeezed, you expect to get... lemon juice

When you see an orange squeezed, you expect to get... orange juice

When you see a Christian squeezed, you should expect to see... Christ

I don't know what your experience is. I hope we all have people we can walk with through difficult times and see the love and the grace and the hope and the confidence of Christ as they are put through the press.

But in my experience that's unfortunately, very few people. It's my goal to help change that.

I've asked Christians "What to get when you squeeze a Christian..." and once they realize it's not the setup for a joke, they'll usually respond "un-christian" and then explain that must mean people who said they were Christian weren't really Christian to begin with.

I'm reluctant to agree. Mainly because I've been squeezed and Christ hasn't always oozed out. And all that means to me is I need to deepen my relationship with Him. The world needs to see more Jesus in me.

We all need this

Would it surprise you to know that as I was preparing for one year's Negativity Fast, I was coming under a huge conviction that I needed to take my own advice? I was setting up the blog posts and as I was reading what I wrote I realized...

- I was agreeing with my circumstances instead of agreeing with the Word of God.
- I was choosing to be offended.
- I was holding on to bitterness as if I had a right to it.
- I was refusing to forgive because "those people should know better".

I had to go apologize to my wife and my kids and God and ask them all for forgiveness.

The Father of Lies enjoys getting us focussed on the lies that we tell ourselves or that others told us in the past, and if we're not intentional about our thoughts, we can easily agree with the enemy.

Do you need proof from Scripture? Matthew 16:13-24 (NLT)

> When Jesus came to the region of Caesarea Philippi, he asked his disciples, "Who do people say that the Son of Man is?" "Well," they replied,

> "some say John the Baptist, some say Elijah, and others say Jeremiah or one of the other prophets." Then he asked them, "But who do you say I am?" Simon Peter answered, "You are the Messiah, the Son of the living God." Jesus replied, "You are blessed, Simon son of John, because my Father in heaven has revealed this to you. You did not learn this from any human being.

It was a divine revelation. Peter had heard from God. He had that connection with the divine. Peter was speaking God's thoughts and truth... Now jump down three verses to verse 21.

> From then on Jesus began to tell his disciples plainly that it was necessary for him to go to Jerusalem, and that he would suffer many terrible things at the hands of the elders, the leading priests, and the teachers of religious law. He would be killed, but on the third day he would be raised from the dead. But Peter took him aside and began to reprimand him for saying such things. "Heaven forbid, Lord," he said. "This will never happen to you!" Jesus turned to Peter and said, "Get away from me, Satan! You are a dangerous trap to me. You are seeing things merely from a human point of view, not from

> God's." Then Jesus said to his disciples, "If any of you wants to be my follower, you must turn from your selfish ways, take up your cross, and follow me.

Five verses after saying the divine relation of who Jesus was, Peter was echoing the temptation Jesus faced in the desert. Satan tempted Jesus to bow down to him and take the easy way to the throne (Matthew 4:8-10). Five verses to move from agreeing with God to agreeing with the enemy. Listen, I know Peter had a different idea of who the Messiah was simply correcting Jesus, so Jesus knew who He was, but he was presenting Jesus with the same option Satan did. And the amazing thing is Peter was still in relationship with Jesus.

How can you not love a God who loves us so much that even when He needs to rebuke us, He doesn't push us away? I want to be like Him.

What Back Surgery Taught Me

I had a time when my back needed surgery. With our health system in Canada, I couldn't see the surgeon for a year and a half. The pain was so intense one day that I couldn't take it. All I could do was stand on a stair with my right leg dangling in the air. I was there for hours. When my wife got home, she took me to the hospital. They gave me a shot of morphine and said they could do nothing else unless it was an emergency - I would know it was an emergency if I lost control of my bowels. Instead, the doctor put me on medication to manage the pain.

He gave me muscle relaxants to stop the back spasms and warned me, "They'll make you sleepy." I was on anti-inflammatory medication to bring down the swelling and they warned me to stay away from ibuprofen, as the anti-inflammatory meds could eat a hole through my stomach. They put me on a narcotic for pain relief. They worked great, but they cautioned me, "Just don't become addicted". Finally, they put on anti–epileptic medication to deaden the nerve receptors. This was my favourite warning: "This could shut down the white blood cells, so see your doctor bi-weekly for blood work and to check for the signs of an ulcer."

It was during this time I had an epiphany - and no; I don't think it was the drugs. My doctors were treating my symptoms, but—barring a miracle—unless they dealt the cause of my pain with through surgery, the treatments, meant to manage the symptoms,could do me much more harm. That's not the epiphany. It's how they explained my situation to me.

The epiphany came when I understood this is what we often do in the church.

We teach preachers to preach to the "felt-need" which is never the root of the problem.

I could no longer give three points and a poem or leave the sermon with people impressed with the PowerPoint presentation. I needed to find the root problems and figure out how to heal the root wounds.

When people are going through the garbage of living in a fallen world, they don't need slogans and bumper sticker theology. They don't even always need answers. What we require is an encounter with the Father and his love.

It's my prayer that you have that encounter with the Father and his love as you journey through these daily readings and fast from negativity.

Not Original with Me

The negativity fast concept is not original with me. I know churches like Bethel in Redding, California, have led people through it. My interest in fasting from negativity came as a response to a prophetic vision a friend in our church experienced.

She saw a giant wave of criticism about to crash on our city and church. It would seek to divide churches, leaders, congregations, friendships and marriages. Now this happens all around us, but I agreed with her sense that what was coming was to be bigger than simply more of the same. I told her to tell our pastor. After all, it's one of his jobs to protect the congregation.

But in the service that followed, God was palpable and as I was interceding for Pastor Kevin, the words "Negativity Fast" came to my mind. I knew little about it and so I did some research.

To my shock, an online search for "negativity fast" brought up business gurus and New Age practitioners selling dubious products, but no references for Christians fasting from negativity. How could this be?

We're the only ones with reasons not to be negative beyond "when you're positive, those around you will be positive" and "studies show positive people make more money and live longer." Hope is the helmet of our salvation. That means there can be no such thing as a pessimistic follower of Christ. We need to be positive because Christ is not negative.

But there are lies we believe that tell us we are the exception. Sometimes what we endure makes it difficult to believe God is good and in a good mood. There are situations that make it seem impossible to abstain from being negative.

The good news is that with either plenty of want, in Christ, you can do all things.

As I studied what the Bible said, and prayed about what to do, God led me to approach my pastor with the idea of a "negativity fast." I would send out daily encouraging emails for 40 days. Every week, I'd produce and syndicate a podcast.

Whenever I could, I'd write articles on various aspects of living above negativity.

Pastor Kevin showed great trust in allowing me to do this. Thanks my friend, you have birthed more dreams in me. We had a few other churches join us immediately. A number more asked for the material for future campaigns.

This book allows you to go through your own negativity fast. It's always better if you can do this as a group, but there is significant benefit even doing it solo. There's not much that you may not already know—except perhaps how to put it into practice. This is a tool for you to do just that.

Trevor H. Lund – Content Creator at RevTrev.com, Founder of Live LIGHT Academy on LiveLIGHT.ca, and completely connectable on TrevorLund.com. As an author and creative, his passion is to help you enjoy peace and joy and hope at all times and in every situation.

TIPS AND TOOLS TO FAST FROM NEGATIVITY

Are you looking to make a difference in the attitudes and actions in your everyday world? Get these Free Tips and Tools to help you Fast from Negativity. They are yours when you sign up today on Live LIGHT Academy.

Here's what you learn:

How do you get rid of self- condemnation or change a negative environment?

How can you rise above discouragement and not crush others with negative words?

How do you judge others properly and do you know you may be living offended at God?

How can you forgive the unforgivable, and can you really stop feeling busy?

What's the best way to confront and can you fight with HONOUR? Learn also how you can stop the worry today.

With tips and tools and answers to FAQ's about Negativity Fasts, get what you need to move from crippling negativity to life-giving positivity today all for free!

Sign up today

https://livelight.ca/tips

LIVE LIGHT ABOVE THE NEGATIVITY COURSE

Move from being easily regularly frustrated, usually feeling busy, often afraid or easily angered TO having peace at all times and in every situation.

Learn to Live LIGHT Above the Negativity with your whole heart.

You were created to walk with God in the garden in the cool of the day. Sin came into the world, and you bore the consequences. Jesus came and took your place and reversed the curse and offered you His yoke that is easy and His burden that is light. You're a child of God creation longs to be revealed. Will you not conform but be transformed, so you can have peace at all times and in every situation?

But what if...

...you're surrounded by negativity?

...you can't control the thoughts in your head?

...you seem more and more on the boiling point of anger?

That's where the **Live LIGHT Above the Negativity Course** comes in.

This course will help you move from being easily regularly frustrated, usually feeling busy, often afraid or easily angered TO having peace at all times and in every situation.

It does this by helping you align your thoughts, your emotions and your actions, so you can Live LIGHT Above the Negativity with your whole heart.

Explore what's inside and choose to Live LIGHT Above the Negativity today! **http://revtrev.link/bless**

What people have said:

> I'm so glad I went through Live LIGHT Above the Negativity course. I feel like it was divinely arranged at the time that I needed it the most. I have read books, but I really enjoyed this course! Throughout the course Trevor repeated it's not about information, but about transformation. The resources that were

provided along with each lesson are very helpful in the transformation process. - Belinda M.

Learn more and join now **http://revtrev.link/bless**

STEP 1: HOW TO FAST FROM NEGATIVITY

DAY 1

REFLECTION

I control my thoughts. My Father has given me everything I need for life and godliness. His Holy Spirit empowers me to accomplish every good work prompted by faith. I take my thoughts captive. I tear down strongholds. I demolish arguments that set themselves up against the knowledge of Christ. I do it with the same power that raised Christ from the dead.

Reflection Question:

Have I been taking thoughts captive or have thoughts been taking me captive lately?

CONTROL YOUR THOUGHTS

DEVOTIONAL

Surely God is good to Israel, to those who are pure in heart. But as for me, my feet had almost slipped; I had nearly lost my foothold. For I envied the arrogant when I saw the prosperity of the wicked. Psalm 73:1-2 (NIV ©2011)

Thought

Are you looking to what God has done and is doing or do you only see what He hasn't yet done? Do you choose to be thankful? Do you choose to agree with the promises of God despite what you experience? Do you choose to live unoffended at God?

I've found over the years that the biggest struggle for overcoming negativity is believing that you have a choice to be positive. I'm not talking about slapping a smile on your face. I'm talking about controlling what you think about. Jesus said, "For the mouth speaks what the heart is full of." (Matthew 12:34 NIV)

We've already agreed that we reap what we sow, right? The same principle is with our thought life. For you programmers out there, maybe you understand "garbage in - garbage out". It's a universal principle. That's why Paul said:

> Finally, brothers and sisters, whatever is true, whatever is noble, whatever is right, whatever is pure, whatever is lovely, whatever is admirable—if anything is excellent or praiseworthy—think about such things. Whatever you have learned or received or heard from me, or seen in me—put it into practice. And the God of peace will be with you. Philippians 4:8-9 (NIV ©2011)

God will help you, but you may need to make the choice to think about what you think about.

Prayer

Lord, help us think about what we think about and choose to think about what you think about us. Show us how to worry about nothing, pray about everything and thank you in all things. In Jesus' name, amen.

Challenge

Will you choose to think about the things Paul tells us to think about? Will you stop thinking negative thoughts?

Declaration

I choose to fast from negativity. I take thoughts captive; I tear down strongholds; I demolish arguments that set themselves up against the knowledge of Christ.

DAY 2

Reflection

I am not my own; I have been bought with a price. I belong to God. His opinion of me is the only opinion that matters. He is for me and not against me. Since he is for me, who can be against me?

Reflection Question:

How does God's opinion of me change my opinion of myself today?

KNOW YOUR IDENTITY

DEVOTIONAL

They have no struggles; their bodies are healthy and strong. They are free from common human burdens; they are not plagued by human ills. Therefore pride is their necklace; they clothe themselves with violence. From their callous hearts comes iniquity; their evil imaginations have no limits. They scoff, and speak with malice; with arrogance they threaten oppression. Their mouths lay claim to heaven, and their tongues take possession of the earth. Therefore their people turn to them and drink up waters in abundance. They say, "How would God know? Does the Most High know anything?" This is what the wicked are like— always free of care, they go on amassing wealth. Surely in vain I have kept my heart pure and have washed my hands in innocence. All day long I have been afflicted, and every morning brings new punishments. Psalm 73:4-14 (NIV ©2011)

Thought

Let's be honest. You don't have to raise your hand, but be honest with yourself... how often do we compare ourselves to others and only see what we lack? The only way to break that thinking off is to know **whose you are** and **who you are**. You need to know... not just in your head, but in your heart. You need to know your identity.

I've got a tool set up at **https://livelight.ca/tips**. You can print off a personalized Identity in Christ. You should go there and sign up for the **Tips and Tools to Fast from Negativity** for free. Print it off your personalized Identity in Christ and memorize it.

But just like Peter had the revelation of who Jesus was, you need to have the revelation of who you are. It's not enough to memorize truth, you need to experience that truth. You need to know you're accepted and you need to know you're a child of God. You need to know the Father heart of God.

You need to know that adoption is an event, not just a position. You need to know He's for you, not against you. You need to know He's good all the time. You need to know this, not just hold it as an idea in your head or a sentiment in your heart. You need to know that you know that you know this.

That comes by spending time with God. That's why we do it for over 46 days.

It starts by replacing the lies you believe about yourself with the truth God says about you.

Prayer

Lord, help us know your opinion of us matters more than our opinion of ourselves or anyone else's opinion of us. Give us a greater revelation of your great love for us. May we know better how wide, how long, how high, and how deep your love is. Amen.

Challenge

Go and sign up or login at **https://revtrev.link/tips** and print off your personalized identity in Christ.

Declaration

I choose to fast from negativity. I take thoughts captive; I tear down strongholds; I demolish arguments that set themselves up against the knowledge of Christ.

DAY 3

REFLECTION

I only let encouragement come out of my mouth. I do my best to always build up and not tear down others. I ask the tough questions Holy Spirit prompts me to, but I speak the truth in love with his help as well. People look to me as a person of wisdom.

Reflection Question:

Have I spoken words I need to apologize for lately?

WATCH YOUR WORDS

DEVOTIONAL

If I had spoken out like that, I would have betrayed your children. When I tried to understand all this, it troubled me deeply. Psalm 73:15-16 (NIV ©2011)

Thought

Two-thirds of the psalms are Psalms of Lament. Most of those are personal songs. They didn't originate to be sung by the community. I enjoy going through the Psalms until I get to one that speaks my situation and how I feel. Then I camp out there for a while and meditate on what's in it.

God isn't interested in masks. In Ancient Greece, the actors wore masks. The actors were called "hypocratis." It's where we get our word hypocrite. God isn't interested in us play-acting before Him. He's given us language in His word...especially the Psalms...that we can use to pour out our emotions to Him.

But that doesn't mean we share our struggles with everyone. Yes, we need people who will walk along with us (Galatians 6:2) (and husbands you need to let your wives share their feelings, and wives don't judge your husband when he finally shares his feelings) but at the same time we don't want to do or say anything that causes someone else to stumble (1 Corinthians 10:32-33). Recognize that:

> Life and death is in the power of the tongue.
> (Proverbs 18:21).

I've seen a philosophy rise in churches that says "Be Real, Be Transparent". How I've seen that worked through is that we share struggles without victory, we share sin without repentance, and my fallen state overrules who I am in Christ.

The Psalmist said it "If I had spoken out like that I would have betrayed your children."

The Psalm is ascribed to Asaph. We don't know exactly what that means. It could be in the style of Asaph, by Asaph, by the sons of Asaph...It's not really important. David assigned the sons of Asaph to prophesy "to the accompaniment of lyres, harps, and cymbals" (1 Chronicles 25:1-2). It's safe to say that the person who had these thoughts and put them to song was a person of authority. He had some influence.

He wrote: "If I had spoken out like that I would have betrayed your children."

You have influence. You influence your family. You influence your workplace. You influence your friends. You influence your church. You influence your small group. You influence everyone who God has placed around you to have influence with.

You serve the One who spoke "Peace" and the storm settled. He's in you to do the same with the storms of life that others have. Never forget -

> Life and death is in the power of the tongue. (Proverbs 18:21).

Too often we forget that, and we use the phrase "That's just how I feel" to justify talking off a godly filter from our mouth. But look what Paul says in Ephesians 4:2— read how the Amplified version puts it:

> Let no foul or polluting language, nor evil word nor unwholesome or worthless talk [ever] come out of your mouth, but only such [speech] as is good and beneficial to the spiritual progress of others, as is fitting to the need and the occasion, that it may be a blessing and give grace (God's favor) to those who hear it. (AMP)

The NIV puts it this way:

> Do not let any unwholesome talk come out of your mouths, but only what is helpful for building others up according to their needs, that it may benefit those who listen.

We are responsible for our tongues. You need to decide how you're going to use your tongue. It's a choice. It's a decision of your will. You can train yourself to only speak the words of life. But it's not a simple thing to change.

Get people around you to help you. Put an elastic band around your wrist and snap it if you have to. You can change the words that come out of your mouth. Holy Spirit empowers you to accomplish every good work prompted by faith. As long you as you control your tongue in faith believing its God's will for you and He'll accomplish it, you will change.

Now what if you're around people who don't choose to speak only the words that build up others?

1. You're responsible for your tongue.

2. Look past what they say to see the wound they're reacting to.

3. Ask God to show His love through you to them.

Prayer

Lord, we need your help to control our tongues. I thank you for giving us everything we need for life and godliness. I thank you for empowering us to accomplish every good work prompted by faith. I thank you that you will finish the good work you started in us and we can trust you'll finish the good work you've started in others. Help us be more like you. Amen.

Challenge

Pour out your emotions to God. Start reading in the Psalms and keep reading until you get to one that matches what you're feeling. Then meditate on it and learn what Holy Spirit is teaching you. strongholds;

Declaration

I choose to fast from negativity. I take thoughts captive; I tear down strongholds; I demolish arguments that set themselves up against the knowledge of Christ.

DAY 4

Reflection

Others see my good works and glorify my Father in heaven. My light shines bright. It's his light others see in me. The darker the night, the brighter my light. I do the good he tells me to do. I do it unto him. I do it all in love.

Reflection Question:

Have others seen His light in me lately?

Consider Your Actions

Devotional

...till I entered the sanctuary of God; then I understood their final destiny. Surely you place them on slippery ground; you cast them down to ruin. How suddenly are they destroyed, completely swept away by terrors! They are like a dream when one awakes; when you arise, Lord, you will despise them as fantasies. Psalm 73:17-20 (NIV ©2011)

Thought

Do you see what our actions bring us? We reap what we sow. Paul wrote to the Galatians:

> Do not be deceived: God cannot be mocked. A man reaps what he sows. Whoever sows to please their flesh, from the flesh will reap destruction;

> whoever sows to please the Spirit, from the Spirit will reap eternal life. Let us not become weary in doing good, for at the proper time we will reap a harvest if we do not give up. Galatians 6:7-9 (NIV ©2011)

God isn't a God of lists and rules. When He tells us how to live, it's because He knows the consequences of our actions when we don't live that way. He loves us too much to allow us to hurt ourselves and others without consequences.

We need to realize we become what we worship (see Psalm 115:8).

I read a blog post about Brad Pitt's spiritual journey. He was raised in a Christian home but couldn't reconcile why God wants us to worship Him. How can God be God and still want our worship? Apparently Brad saw this as God on an ego trip and so chose to believe God doesn't exists.

I'm praying that the Holy Spirit can have someone get through to him that God wants our worship not because He needs an ego boost but because we become what we worship.

By the way, God looks for worshippers, not worship (John 14:23). The difference is dramatic.

The evil ones that the Psalmist was lamenting about weren't worshipping God and the Psalmist realized what their end would be.

You and I can't allow anything in our lives that is contrary to God's will for us. Too often we mistake God's grace with His approval. Let me give you an obvious example:

Out of 29 of the most prominent prayers of the Bible that God said "no" to, over half (17) of the no's to prayers were because of sin in that individual or the people as a whole. Scripture tells us God will not listen to our prayers if...

- We have unconfessed sin. Psalms 66:18
- We live in sin. Isaiah 59:2; John 9:31
- We don't give God our best. Malachi 1:7-9.
- We've turned from God. Jeremiah14:10,12.
- We've rejected His correction. Proverbs 1:24,25,28
- We ignore His precepts. Proverbs 28:9; Zechariah 7:11-13
- We ignore the poor. Proverbs 21:13
- We attack the innocent. Isaiah 1:15
- We put other gods before Him. Jeremiah 11:11-14; Ezekiel 8:15-18.

- We're proud. Job 35:12-13
- We stand in our own righteousness. Luke 18:11-14.
- We're an enemy of His people. Psalms 18:40-41; Miciah. 3.2-4
- We're godless. Job 27:8-9

But I know people who justify their sin because God still answers their prayers. They've mistaken the grace of God with His approval.

Don't be someone like that. You are a new creation in Christ. Live up to what you've already attained (Philippians 3:16).

The psalmist was changed when he went to worship God. We're changed when our focus changes to worship. So as you worship God daily... if you pick up a book and read it as part of your devotion; if you download a Bible Reading Plan and take 46 days just to listen to God... Will you take this season to draw near to God?

Because I know when you do He draws near to you (James 4:8) and when He draws near we're changed, and we become more like the One we worship.

Prayer

Lord, you only did what you saw the Father do and only said what you heard the Father say. Help us do that as well. Help us to be more and more like you. Amen.

Challenge

Can you look God in the eye? Ask Holy Spirit what he think about your actions. Wait to hear what he will say. *Will you choose to get rid of all the actions that hurt you and others?*

Declaration

I choose to fast from negativity. I take thoughts captive, I tear down strongholds, I demolish arguments that set themselves up against the knowledge of Christ.

DAY 5

REFLECTION

I positively change my everyday world. People comment on my smile, laugh and gentle way. I choose gratitude and show appreciation whenever I find it appropriate. I look for when it can be appropriate. I speak the truth in love as a step of faith and know Holy Spirit empowers me to accomplish it.

Reflection Question:

Have I been making a positive difference in my everyday world lately?

CHANGE YOUR ENVIRONMENT

DEVOTIONAL

When my heart was grieved and my spirit embittered, I was senseless and ignorant; I was a brute beast before you. Yet I am always with you; you hold me by my right hand. You guide me with your counsel, and afterward you will take me into glory.
Psalm 73:21-24 (NIV ©2011)

Thought

When we worship God good things happen. That's when our perspective changes. This is what happened to the Psalmist - verses 21-24.

When you connect with God on a personal and daily basis, He's going to show you the things in your life He wants to change. He's going to teach you how to avoid bitterness. He's going to give you tools to forgive others and live unoffended at God.

There is a better way to live. You can change your environment instead of being changed by it. You serve the One who spoke peace to the storm. You are someone who can do the same.

I've had an atheist friend run up to me and say, "You need to pray for me. I need peace." It's a good day whenever an atheist runs up to you and asks for prayer.

Where do you start?

It starts by controlling what you can control and letting God take care of the rest. You can choose not to become bitter. You can choose to forgive. You can choose to live unoffended at God.

This is what the psalmist did. He admitted his pain and how he reacted because of it. And he didn't dwell on his failures; he moved on to God's goodness. Will you move on to God's goodness?

Prayer

Lord, we need your supernatural empowering to change our everyday world. It's you who change it through us, help us not to get in the way. Help us shine your light and draw people to you. Amen.

Challenge

Will you choose to change your environment? Start by choosing to bless and not curse.

Declaration

I choose to fast from negativity. I take thoughts captive; I tear down strongholds; I demolish arguments that set themselves up against the knowledge of Christ.

DAY 6

Reflection

I take time to be in awe of my Creator. Whether it's listening to worship music that reminds me of his presence in the here and now, or it's enjoying nature or mathematics or history or anything else that he's created for his glory. I will be still and know that HE is God.

Reflection Question:

Have I taken time to be in awe of God lately?

FOCUS ON GOD

DEVOTIONAL

Whom have I in heaven but you? And earth has nothing I desire besides you. My flesh and my heart may fail, but God is the strength of my heart and my portion forever. Those who are far from you will perish; you destroy all who are unfaithful to you. But as for me, it is good to be near God. I have made the Sovereign LORD my refuge; I will tell of all your deeds. Psalm 73:25-28 (NIV©2011)

Thought

The psalm ends up - as most Psalms of Laments do - with praise to God.

Oh yah. It's going to be good. I've done this enough to know it's going to be very good. I didn't say easy. Nothing worth doing is ever easy. But it's good.

For most of us, fasting from negativity brings a reaction. Offense rises up in some people. Humility rises up in others. Those who seek after God find Him and good things happen.

I have had people sign up for the daily content who get really upset that they need to change their thoughts, words and actions. Sometimes people say they just can't handle that kind of challenge right now. They'd rather just hold onto their offence. I occasionally get really nasty emails from people who try to justify their negativity. These people are hurt and don't know how to heal and a daily reminder of the choices they've made just isn't going to cut it. They need healing relationships. If that's you, you need a church that is a place to be healed. Get connected and see God put on flesh in the people He connects you to.

Now we've also had some really fun comments from people that I like to share:

> "While I was fasting from negativity, my boss gave me a gift certificate for $100 for being the most positive person in the company." (your results may vary)

> "After the negativity fast, my boss asked what my secret was for looking younger as I got older. I had

to mention giving up negativity." (your results may vary)

There is nothing in what I do to help people fast from negativity that is earth-shattering or purposefully revolutionary. In fact, it's so basic I just met a brand new baby Christian and told her "Go through it..." It's that basic and that foundational.

Many people don't even need the daily reflection and devotional. I make them available because they are good tools and they lend themselves to a community event.

But...

- If you choose today to watch your thoughts, so you only think about whatever is true, whatever is noble, whatever is right, whatever is pure, whatever is lovely, whatever is admirable— excellent or praiseworthy.
- If you choose today to use your tongue only speaks the words of life.
- If you choose today to stop doing everything you know God doesn't want you to do because it's hurtful to you and others.
- If you choose today to change your negative environment instead of reacting to it.

Then get on with it.

You've got the Holy Spirit to teach you all things (John 14:26). Life up to what you've already attained. Be the agents of change your city, your country and our world needs.

Prayer

Lord, help us to keep our focus on your empowering grace to help us on this journey. We need you for everything we need for life and godliness. Thank you that you're always with us, help us all to be with you. Amen

Challenge

How has the first week been for you? Let us know what God is doing. **http://revtrev.link/mystory**

Declaration

I choose to fast from negativity. I take thoughts captive, I tear down strongholds, I demolish arguments that set themselves up against the knowledge of Christ.

STEP 2: BE PREPARED FOR YOUR ENEMY

DAY 7

Reflection

I take up my position, stand firm and see the deliverance that comes from the Lord. I humble myself under his mighty hand, and He lifts me up. I pray fervently until the situation changes or I am the one who changes. I know He goes before me and behind me and is within me. This battle is not mine, it's the Lord's.

Reflection Question:

When was the last time I prayed until the situation or I changed?

PREPARE FOR BATTLE

DEVOTIONAL

Finally, be strong in the Lord and in his mighty power. Put on the full armour of God so that you can take your stand against the devil's schemes. For our struggle is not against flesh and blood, but against the rulers, against the authorities, against the powers of this dark world and against the spiritual forces of evil in the heavenly realms. Ephesians 6 :10-12 (NIV)

Thought

When the children of Israel entered the promise land, it was to engage in battle with the enemies whose sin reached its full measure (Genesis 15:16). When they entered the land flowing with milk and honey, it wasn't a holiday. It wasn't time to relax. It was time to engage the enemy.

And the time for us to do the same is now.

Our enemy isn't flesh and blood and God is good, so He hasn't called us to do something He hasn't already equipped us for.

God has provided us armour and "putting it on" is more than just saying, "I have put on the full armour of God!" Having the armour of God on is living out its implications for our lives.

Living with the armour of God in place is what we're going to be reminded of this first week as we refrain from any thought or talk that is contrary to the will of God expressed in Scripture.

Prayer

Lord, thank You for preparing us for every battle that we face. Thank You that You never leave us or forsake us. Thank You, You've called us your partners and co-workers and friends. Help us, Holy Spirit, to be overwhelmed with that once more.

Challenge

We prepare ourselves to allow God to change us and a vocal declaration of truth opens the way for that to begin. Just by saying, "I have put on the full armour of God!" doesn't mean we have... but it does mean we're willing. It's not a magic formula, but it has the power to break down thoughts that set themselves up against the knowledge of God.

The challenge today should be easy for most, but some may find it a little silly or trite. Watch your judgmental attitude. When we're teachable, God can do miracles.

Today's challenge is to vocalize the declaration today and every day this week we are reminded to have the full armour of God in place. Then thank God for His Goodness in preparing you for every battle. Thank Him by faith if you can't see it in the moment.

Declaration

I choose to put on the full armour of God. I put on truth. I put on righteousness. I put on peace. I put on faith. I put on salvation. And I choose to learn to use the word of God with great power and in love.

DAY 8

REFLECTION

I am not my own. I have been bought with a price. I belong to God. It's His life that now lives in me. I let my "'yes" be "yes" and my "no" be "no". I keep my word, even when it hurts. I do everything as working unto the Lord. His Holy Spirit prompts me and empowers me today and every day.

Reflection Question:

Have I been tempted to not be a person of my word lately?

BE REAL

DEVOTIONAL

Again I say, don't get involved in foolish, ignorant arguments that only start fights. A servant of the Lord must not quarrel but must be kind to everyone, be able to teach, and be patient with difficult people. 2 Timothy 2:23-24 (NLT)

Thought

Paul is describing the uniform of a Roman Legionnaire in Ephesians 6. A soldier would be wearing a hanging tunic. It would have a belt around the middle to keep it flaps out-of-the-way and the outfit in place.

Derek Prince taught on the belt of truth that "We are to put away sham, clichés, religious hypocrisy, saying words that are just cop-outs and stop saying what we don't even believe. We can't just 'hang'."

We must be real. But real doesn't mean "fallen" - in Christ that's not who you are.

The Greek verb tenses in Ephesians 6:14, 15 is lost in the NIV, but trust me; it has three of the pieces of armour already on you. The belt, breastplate and shoes represent the parts of your protection you were given when you receive Jesus Christ. In them, you are commanded to stand firm.

The Greek tense of the verb suggests the action it refers to was completed before we were commanded to stand firm. A Roman soldier would put on his belt, breastplate and shoes before trying to stand. In the same way, we are to put on the full armour of God after having already put on Christ. If you haven't made Jesus your Lord, this is meaningless.

But when you have made Jesus your Lord, we choose to live in truth and integrity. We should be in "place" with truth.

Are you?

Do you let your "yes" be "yes" and your "no", "no"? (see James 5:12) Do you keep your word, even when it hurts? (see Psalm 15:1-4) Do you speak the truth in love when you speak the truth? (see Ephesians 4:15)

And you thought a fast from negativity was going to be an easy challenge.

Prayer

Lord, I confess I have not always been a person of my word, but I thank You, that with Your help, I can be starting now. Holy Spirit, convict me whenever I exaggerate even a little; tell me when I'm taking on more than I can honestly accomplish. Help me to keep my word, even when it hurts. I want people to know I'm happy to represent You.

Challenge

Guard your conversation today and have integrity with who Christ has called you to be. You may need to confess exaggeration that makes you look better than you are or another one worse than they were.

Declaration

I choose to put on the full armour of God. I put on truth. I put on righteousness. I put on peace. I put on faith. I put on salvation. And I choose to learn to use the word of God with great power and in love.

DAY 9

Reflection

I am loved. I live loved. No greater love is there than to lay down your life for another. Christ laid down his life for me. I lay down my life for my loved ones. His love is in me and empowers me to love - not only those I love - but those I find it difficult to love. I lived loved because I am loved.

Reflection Question:

Who have I shown love to lately? Was it easy or not so easy?

Above All Else, Guard Your Heart

Devotional

Above all else, guard your heart, for it is the wellspring of life.
Proverbs 4:23 (NIV)

Thought

The breastplate protects the heart. The Breastplate of Righteousness described by Paul in Ephesians 6 is not from works gained from the Law (Philippians 3:9) but it is the righteousness of Christ we put on by faith (2 Corinthians 5:21). 1 Thessalonians uses the same motif of a breastplate and describes it as faith and love.

> But since we belong to the day, let us be self-controlled, putting on faith and love as a breastplate, and the hope of salvation as a helmet. 1 Thessalonians 5:8 (NIV)

Our own righteousness isn't going to cut it. In fact, if we work out of our own righteousness, satan can easily penetrate our breastplate and get to our heart. The breastplate of righteousness works in an active faith in Christ that works through love.

Over this fast from negativity you're going to be reading much about love, because love is the antidote to negativity.

Love guards our heart. It protects what is most important. It reflects the nature of God.

The Breastplate of Righteousness protects our heart, which is the symbolic centre of our love. It's Christ's righteousness, which is His love shown to us. So as we accept His love and we respond to His love, we protect our capacity to love.

So are you ready to show Christ's love to others?

Prayer

Lord, help me to put the needs of others ahead of my own. Help me to do everything in love. Empower me to live beyond my limited sphere of selfishness. Help me to love others because You first loved me. Amen.

Challenge

Pray for opportunity to show God's love to someone today. Then respond to those you meet with love.

Declaration

I choose to put on the full armour of God. I put on truth. I put on righteousness. I put on peace. I put on faith. I put on salvation. And I choose to learn to use the word of God with great power and in love.

DAY 10

Reflection

I look for opportunities to share Jesus and his love. I am prepared to give an answer when people ask about the hope I have. I want people to know about what Jesus has done in my life. His peace and joy and hope are evident, and I am excited when people ask me about it.

Reflection Question:

Am I active in sharing my faith? When was the last time I talked to someone about Jesus?

Are You Quick to See God's Will Done?

Devotional

I pray that you may be active in sharing your faith, so that you will have a full understanding of every good thing we have in Christ. Philemon 1:6 (NIV)

Thought

The shoes described in Ephesians 6 were strong, heavy sandals that were durable and provided mobility and availability to the commander. In our case, our commander is Jesus.

We need to be prepared to have an intelligent account of the Gospel. So many Christians don't even understand the basics of the Gospel. The kerygma (message) of Paul is straightforward –

Jesus Christ has come in the flesh He died for our sins, was crucified, buried and raised from the dead, He ascended to heaven and will one day return to judge the living and the dead so repent!

It is a Gospel of Peace. We can only transfer peace to others if we have it ourselves. If we don't have peace, then it's no use trying to give it to someone else. If you need peace, meditate on, and put into practice Isaiah 26:3, Romans 15:13 and Philippians 4:6-9.

Erwin McManus has an incredible story about a radio talk show host asking him: "So are everyone but Christians going to hell?"

He responded with something similar to, "Let me be up-front, I am a follower of Christ and know that He said He is the way to the Father. But He also didn't come into the world to condemn the world, so that's not something I can do either."

I enjoy Erwin's thinking because it's similar to my own. I was speaking to a Comparative Religions Class at a local university about the early church councils. It led beautifully into the question, "Is Jesus God?" I asked, "Have you ever been offended by someone telling you Jesus is the only way?" All but three were quick to agree.

I responded, "I'm a follower of Jesus and I ask you for forgiveness for others who name His name and use His words to condemn you. I'm sorry."

That got their attention, so I continued, "It would be perfectly legitimate to feel offended at Jesus, if He was just a man, and He said, 'I am the way, the truth and the life.' But what if He was more than a man? What if He was the one who put 400 million stars in our galaxy and 400 million galaxies in our universe, and who knows how many more universes there are left to imagine? It would mean He wasn't being exclusive when He said He was the way, it would mean He was being inclusive, making a way where we couldn't make one on our own."

If the teacher wasn't a Muslim, I would have tried an altar call. People respond to a gospel of peace.

Having your shoes on means often doing for God right there what He tells you to do. You obey without hesitation. You don't stall in communicating the Gospel of Peace in a way that meets people's needs right there and then.

Are you ready to put into practice the will of God expressed in Scripture?

Prayer

Lord, I know You want me to be active in sharing my faith. I know You're not willing that any should perish. I know You will tell me what to say. I know You want my conversation full of grace seasoned with salt, so I'll know how to answer everyone. Thank You, Holy Spirit, for empowering me to be Christ's witness. Empower me to make the most of every opportunity today to plant, water, or harvest Your word. I'll do it all for the glory of God. Amen.

Challenge

Find someone to share the Gospel of Peace with today. Pray knowing it's God's will for you to share your faith. Pray believing the Holy Spirit will teach you what to say. Then share your stories with us... **http://revtrev.link/mystory**

Declaration

I choose to put on the full armour of God. I put on truth. I put on righteousness. I put on peace. I put on faith. I put on salvation. And I choose to learn to use the word of God with great power and in love.

DAY 11

REFLECTION

Faith is my natural response to His revelation. It's a gift He gives me. It's a muscle I exercise. Faith without works is dead. I prove my faith by the good works He shines before people to see. Faith is the shield that protects me. Faith is one of the three that remain.

Reflection Question:

Do people see my good works and glorify my Father in heaven?

TESTING OUR FAITH

DEVOTIONAL

But if they had stood in my council, they would have proclaimed my words to my people and would have turned them from their evil ways and from their evil deeds. Jeremiah 23:22 (NIV)

Thought

Without faith, it's impossible to please God (Hebrews 11:6) because everything not done by faith is sin (Romans 14:23).

Faith is our obedient response to hearing the voice of God.

Faith is what protects us; it is our shield. The Roman shield covered everything the soldier was responsible for. So too, our faith covers us. Faith is an excellent verb and a debilitating noun.

Faith comes by hearing and hearing by the present-spoken words of God (Romans 10:17).

How do we know what we're responsible for until we read it in the Bible, or it's quickened in our Spirits?

What this means is we need to regularly have some quiet time with God. My brother-in-law coined my favourite term for it : "shut-up and listen time."

Jesus was pronounced "Immanuel" – God with us. We don't live in the 400 years before John, when God didn't speak to His people. We don't live in a time before Samuel when the word of God was rare. We are in a relationship with the One who spoke the worlds into being. Because of the blood of Christ we have direct access to the Father. Because of the Holy Spirit, we are empowered to communicate with God beyond our understanding. God still speaks to us today.

John 15:15 tells us that because we obey God, we are friends with Christ, no longer servants because servants don't know the plans of their Master. But Jesus lets us know what he learns from the Father.

Do we take the time to listen? When we listen, we can walk by faith. When we don't take time to listen, is it really faith we're walking in?

When you come before Him, quiet your Spirit, focus on His love and expect Him to speak, He does!

And He still speaks the words of life today (John 6:8). He speaks peace to the storms and there is fullness of joy in His presence. When we quiet ourselves and invite Him to speak, He will. When we're quick to obey – that's faith.

Test it and see.

Prayer

Father, I come in the name of Jesus Christ with thanksgiving and praise and as I wait expectantly upon You now, I do my best to listen to Your voice. I stand before You, Almighty God and seek Your counsel. Please reveal any information I need; any strategies that I can employ right now so that I can be knowing and doing what You want.

Challenge

Spend some "shut-up and listen time" (quiet time) alone with God today. Finish up your requests and leave time for Him to speak to you. Focus on His love. Cease striving and rest. Expect Him to speak. Some worshipful music can help. If you can't do it for more than two minutes, take a scripture and think about it from every possible angle with the love of God in full view.

Declaration

I choose to put on the full armour of God. I put on truth. I put on righteousness. I put on peace. I put on faith. I put on salvation. And I choose to learn to use the word of God with great power and in love.

DAY 12

Reflection

My hope is real. It does not disappoint. My hope is not in potential or circumstance, it is in the person of my risen Lord. Because He lives, the best is yet to come! Because he goes before and behind me and is within me, my hope is real!

Reflection Question:

Have disappointments hardened my heart to hope?

Hope That Is Real

Devotional

But since we belong to the day, let us be self-controlled, putting on faith and love as a breastplate, and the hope of salvation as a helmet. 1 Thessalonians 5:8 (NIV)

Thought

The helmet of salvation protects our mind and 1 Thessalonians 5:8 tells us our mind represents hope. Faith is the substance of things hoped for (Hebrews 11:1) and so real hope can only be built on faith.

Hope is a quiet expectation of the fulfillment of God's promises. In a sense, it is continuous optimism. Hope that is built on faith and negativity can't exist together.

If we believe Romans 8:28, then there is no reason for pessimism, self-pity, doubt, or mistrust ...we are saved by hope.

Hopelessness is the condition of those away from God. It should never be the condition of the Christian because "Christ in us is the hope of glory" (Colossians 1:27).

Hope is an essential part of our Salvation experience. When we have Hope, we are anchored. Hope is optimism.

Hope needs to be seen and so it requires some response to the faith on which it is built. Are you trusting God to be true to His word? Take Psalm 34:19 as an example:

> The righteous person faces many troubles, but
> the Lord comes to the rescue each time.

Are you needing Him to come to the rescue? Then respond to each promise in scripture with praise. It shows the hope that you have.

Prayer

Lord, I am so thankful it is not my righteousness that allows me to stand before You and be called Your child. It is Your righteousness that makes me right in the Father's eyes. Thank You, Lord, I have never seen the righteous forsaken or the children of the righteous begging for bread. Thank You for being our provider. Thank you for You own the cattle on a thousand hills. You are good and don't give Your children a serpent when we need a fish, or a rock when we need bread. Thank You for being trustworthy. Thank You for being worthy.

Challenge

Take some time today to praise God no matter your situation. Praise Him especially if you don't feel like it. Praise Him for who He is. Praise Him for what He's done. Praise Him for what He's promised.

Declaration

I choose to put on the full armour of God. I put on truth. I put on righteousness. I put on peace. I put on faith. I put on salvation. And I choose to learn to use the word of God with great power and in love.

DAY 13

Reflection

I hide his Word in my heart so I don't sin against him. On his Word I meditate day and night. His Word is lamp to my feet and light to my path. I have taken an oath and confirmed it, I follow his righteous word. His word is bread. His word is truth. His word is life. I think about what is good and right and true.

Reflection Question:

Have I allowed His word to read me lately?

When Worry Isn't Negative

Devotional

Your word is a lamp to my feet and a light for my path. I have taken an oath and confirmed it, that I will follow your righteous laws. Psalm 119:105-106 (NIV)

Thought

The sword of the Spirit is the main offensive weapon mentioned in Ephesians 6 – prayer is another. Lies we believe can't stand up to the word of God.

When satan tempted Jesus in the desert, Jesus always responded to the half-truth with the full truth from the word of God. He didn't argue points – he pointed out Scripture.

We need to do the same. To do it effectively we need to have the word of God inside of us. We can't be passive in our knowledge, memorization and meditation of scripture. It's our bread; our life.

Now, most of us who have been on the journey for a while know we can always learn more from the Bible, and we should know the benefits of putting it to memory, but when the Bible says "I meditate..." how do we do that?

If you know how to worry, you know how to meditate. It's like a cow chewing its cud. You think about a passage 100 different ways. You go over it again and again and again and again. It starts to work its way into your being and brings faith with it. It's much like how worry brings fear into your being. Worry is negative because it grows fear. Meditation is positive because it grows faith.

Prayer

Thank you, Lord, for Your word that is able to teach, rebuke, correct and train in righteousness. It is my bread. It is life. Thank You that by it, I know about Your love, creation, friendship, salvation, mercy, grace, peace, assurance, restoration, cleansing, power, wisdom and knowledge. Thank You, Your word is alive and reads me. Speak to me as I read it. May I only read to learn more about You.

Challenge

Pick a passage and meditate on it today. Spend some time in the morning; think about it throughout the day. Consider it on your bed at night. You'll be living the command in Philippians 4:8:

> And now, dear brothers and sisters, one final thing. Fix your thoughts on what is true, and honourable, and right, and pure, and lovely, and admirable. Think about things that are excellent and worthy of praise. (NLT)

Declaration

I choose to put on the full armour of God. I put on truth. I put on righteousness. I put on peace. I put on faith. I put on salvation. And I choose to learn to use the word of God with great power and in love.

STEP 3: LET FRUIT BE FRUIT

DAY 14

Reflection

I grow in the fruit of Spirit. Love and joy and peace and patience and kindness and goodness and faithfulness and self-control all are becoming more and more evident in my life. I notice the difference and others comment on the difference. I am becoming more like Jesus.

Reflection Question:

Have I noticed more of the Spirit's fruit in my life lately?

FRUIT HAPPENS

DEVOTIONAL

You were taught, with regard to your former way of life, to put off your old self, which is being corrupted by its deceitful desires; to be made new in the attitude of your minds; and to put on the new self, created to be like God in true righteousness and holiness. Ephesians 4:22-24 (NIV)

Thought

The Bible is so rich with metaphors that we can see in the natural. When you think about it, how else could the created understand the Creator? We recognize our language and experience is limited by our mortality, but at the same time we realize it is God who has revealed Himself to us.

That thought alone makes me stop and worship. I wish I could relay it more profoundly.

Here's one that makes me go "Aha!"

The moon does not have its own light, but reflects the light of the sun to the part of the world that's away from the light. There are two things that happen to stop the light from the sun being reflected to the world. They both have to do with the position of the moon.

First, the world can come between the moon and sun - whose light it was created to reflect to the part of the world that's away from the sun- it's called a lunar eclipse. The shadow of the world covers the face of the moon that reflects the light of the sun.

Second, the moon is also able to come between the sun and the side of the world that is directly receiving its light. The shadow of the moon covers a portion of the earth instead of reflecting the sun's light to the side of the world that is away from the sun. We call that a solar eclipse.

Finally, there is also a time when the moon is in the perfect position to reflect the greatest amount of the light of the sun, to the part of the world that is away from the sun. It is the brightest, biggest moon of the year, and it happens in the Northern Hemisphere in the Fall.

We happen to call that the "harvest moon."

The same is true for us. We reflect the goodness of God by choosing to grow the fruit of the Spirit that reflects His good nature. It puts us in the position to reflect the greatest amount of His light to the part of the world that is still in darkness.

Love, joy, peace, patience, kindness, goodness, faithfulness, gentleness and self-control together show the nature of Jesus to the world. And there are two truths about fruit we need to be aware of.

The first truth is – fruit happens. Jesus is the vine; we are the branches. When we abide in Him, we bear much fruit. It's as natural as the moon reflecting the light from the sun to the side of the world that's away from the sun. The lesson is abiding in the vine.

The second truth is – we need to tend an orchard. This thought doesn't contradict the first, although I admit I'm mixing metaphors. Growing in the fruit of the Spirit is a choice we make, as well as a series of choices throughout the day. We will constantly need to choose love, joy, peace and patience. We will have an opportunity to choose kindness, goodness and faithfulness. Conditions will be conducive for us to not wish to choose gentleness and self-control.

So does fruit just happen, or do we tend to the tree? Both. Learn how to abide and fruit just happens. Abiding means keeping in step with the rhythms of the Master and in our fallen state, it is a choice to reflect the light of the sun to the side of the world that's away from the sun.

The next few days we'll be encouraged to make that choice a habit.

Prayer

Thank you, Lord, that when I abide in You, Your words abide in me and I can ask whatever I want, and it will be given to me. Teach me to abide. Thank You, Holy Spirit, You will empower me to put on and grow love, joy, peace, patience, kindness, goodness, faithfulness, gentleness and self-control.

Challenge

If you could show God to the world in any way that reflects His goodness and Glory, how would you do it? Pray and obey. There are things you can do today that will see that prayer fulfilled. Do them.

Declaration

I choose to reflect the light of the Son to the side of the world that's away from the Son. I choose to put on love, joy, peace, patience, kindness, goodness, faithfulness, gentleness and self-control.

DAY 15

Reflection

I love because I am first loved. Perfect love casts out fear. Perfect love comes from the Father to me and flows from me to everyone in everyday world. I recognize His love on me and over me and in me, and I am thankful for the great love He entrusts to me.

Reflection Question:

Have I been realizing His love for me lately?

The Antidote to Negativity

Devotional

Love is patient, love is kind. It does not envy, it does not boast, it is not proud. It is not rude, it is not self-seeking, it is not easily angered, it keeps no record of wrongs. Love does not delight in evil but rejoices with the truth. It always protects, always trusts, always hopes, always perseveres. Love never fails. 1 Corinthians 13:4-8 (NIV)

Thought

Love is the antidote to negativity. How can you act in love and speak **Careless words** Matthew 12:35-37 (HCSB); **"Loose" words** Proverbs 10:19 (NIV); **Angry words** James 1:19 (NLT); **Cutting words** Proverbs 12:18 (NLT); **Discouraging words** Numbers 32:7 (NIV); **Untruthful words** Ephesians 4:25 (NIV); **Complaining words** Philippians 2:14-16 (NLT); **Slanderous**

words Ephesians 4:31 (NIV); **Obscene words** Ephesians 5:4 (NIV); **Abusive Words** Ephesians 4:29 (NLT); **Dissenting Words** Proverbs 16:28 (NIV); **Or Gossip**? Proverbs 20:19 (NLT)

You can't.

Love fulfills the law (Romans 13:10). It is the revealed nature of God (1 John 4:16). It is how we are to treat one another (John 13:34-35). It's how we are to behave towards everyone (Luke 10:27).

Yet the word "love" is trite. It's not specific enough. We love our spouse. We love our dog. We love jalapeños in sandwiches. How can we know what love is?

We need to understand love the way God wants us to understand it. We can only define our love by how God loved us:

> This is love: not that we loved God, but that he loved us and sent his Son as an atoning sacrifice for our sins. 1 John 4:10 (NIV)

> Husbands, go all out in your love for your wives, exactly as Christ did for the church—a love marked by giving, not getting. Christ's love makes the church whole. His words evoke her

> beauty. Everything he does and says is designed to bring the best out of her, dressing her in dazzling white silk, radiant with holiness. And that is how husbands ought to love their wives. They're really doing themselves a favour—since they're already "one" in marriage. Ephesians 5:25-28 (The Message)

And we can only measure our love, by the way God measures it:

> This is how we know that we love the children of God: by loving God and carrying out his commands. This is love for God: to obey his commands. And his commands are not burdensome, for everyone born of God overcomes the world. This is the victory that has overcome the world, even our faith. 1 John 5:2-4 (NIV)

So "love" means obedience to God. Love means self-sacrifice. Love means you show it before the other one deserves it. **Have you shown that love to someone today?**

Prayer

Lord, I thank You that Your commands are not burdensome, and I thank You for giving the Holy Spirit to help me in my weakness. I want to reflect Your goodness to people not directly in Your light. Help me show love even before I feel like it, so the love I show can be sincere. Thank You that since this prayer is according to Your will, I know I have what I ask of You.

Challenge

Every time you speak careless, "loose," angry, cutting, discouraging, untruthful, complaining, slanderous, obscene, abusive or dissenting words and gossip, confess it to God and ask the forgiveness of the one you spoke them to. Have grace for others who speak them to you.

Declaration

I choose to reflect the light of the Son to the side of the world that's away from the Son. I choose to put on love, joy, peace, patience, kindness, goodness, faithfulness, gentleness and self-control.

DAY 16

Reflection

The joy of the Lord is my strength. I praise him in the storm. I thank him before the answer comes. His joy bubbles up in me. I celebrate every day. He rejoices over me with singing. It is good to sing praises to him and thank him in all situations. He is my joy.

Reflection Question:

I have felt his joy in my life lately?

Our Strength is No Secret

Devotional

This day is sacred to our Lord. Do not grieve, for the joy of the LORD is your strength. Nehemiah 8:10 (NIV)

Thought

The book of Nehemiah is such a good analogy for our fast from negativity. If I had remembered the story when I first wrote this material, the fast from negativity would have been 52 days, since that's how long it took the people to re-build the walls of Jerusalem to a defensible position and that's a metaphor for what we're doing now.

Those rebuilding the walls endured distraction, ridicule and discouragement. This is what most of us have endured as we rid ourselves of everything contrary to the will of God expressed in Scripture.

Negativity saps our joy, but Nehemiah told the people to stop looking at the situation because "the joy of the Lord is your strength."

Joy, like all the fruit of the Spirit, is a choice. It's something we choose to have despite our situation. Now that's not very practical or encouraging when you're in the middle of disappointment and discouragement. So here's another truth that is more practical:

Joy is something we choose to pursue. David wrote:

> You have made known to me the path of life; you will fill me with joy in your presence, with eternal pleasures at your right hand. Psalm 16:11 (NIV)

We can practice the presence of God and recognize He is everywhere present and find joy in knowing that. We also need to pursue the palpable presence of God, slowing our conversation with Him and taking time to listen to His voice.

And joy can overwhelm us, regardless of the circumstance we face.

Prayer

Lord, I need joy. I need laughter. I need to celebrate the good things that a good God has given me and made for me. Lord, You are good, and You fill me with joy in your presence. Help me to recognize Your presence today. Fill me with joy as I make time to pursue Your palpable presence. Your joy is my strength.

Challenge

Choose joy today. Practice the presence of God – slow down enough to recognize He is everywhere present. Pursue the palpable presence of God - spend some time relaxing in His presence, expecting Him to fill you with joy.

Declaration

I choose to reflect the light of the Son to the side of the world that's away from the sun. I choose to put on love, joy, peace, patience, kindness, goodness, faithfulness, gentleness and self-control.

DAY 17

Reflection

I seek peace at all times and in every situation. Peace guides my steps and guards my emotions. Peace rules in my heart and I am thankful. As far as it depends on me, I live at peace with everyone. Anything that costs me my peace, is too expensive. He is my peace.

Reflection Question:

Have I experienced peace at all times and in every situation lately?

SEEK PEACE AND PURSUE IT

DEVOTIONAL

You will keep in perfect peace all who trust in you, all whose thoughts are fixed on you! Isaiah 26:3 (NLT)

Thought

When we were in New Zealand, everyone was so laid-back compared with what we were used to in North America. When you signalled to change lanes on a busy motorway, people would actually give way to you. It was astounding.

Few were in a hurry. "No worries" is the standard reply. No one seemed busy... unless you were in the church.

I spoke to some of my pastor friends about this: "How can you reach a culture that's laid-back, when you seem to take pride in being busy?" I suppose what I meant was, how can the church teach peace when they don't experience it?

I'm not pointing fingers here. In North America it's so much worse. We add church programs into a busy schedule and feel holiest when we are close to burnout. How can we have "feet fitted with the gospel of peace" when we don't have peace?

But we can have peace. It's our choice to obey God.

We can fix our thoughts on Him (Isaiah 26:3) and take all of our requests to Him with thanksgiving (Philippians 4 :6-8) We can forgive others for our sake and choose to live un-offended at God. We can cease striving and give up our right to understand, so we can have the peace that passes understanding.

So, will you?

Prayer

Lord, in my weakness You are strong, and I need Your strength to help me choose peace. I need Your peace to share Your good news. I need Your peace to calm me in the storm. I need Your peace, so others will see Your goodness and greatness in me. I choose today to seek peace and pursue it.

Challenge

Take everything you are worrying about, and thank God for the answers that are promised in His word. Meditate on Matthew 6:7-34.

Declaration

I choose to reflect the light of the Son to the side of the world that's away from the Son. I choose to put on love, joy, peace, patience, kindness, goodness, faithfulness, gentleness and self-control.

DAY 18

Reflection

As I love, I am patient, I am kind. I am not jealous or boastful or proud or rude. I do not demand my own way. I am not irritable. I keep no record of being wronged. I am interruptible and unoffendable. I am patient.

Reflection Question:

Have I been patient lately?

IS PATIENCE INACTION?

DEVOTIONAL

Dear brothers and sisters, when troubles come your way, consider it an opportunity for great joy. For you know that when your faith is tested, your endurance has a chance to grow. So let it grow, for when your endurance is fully developed, you will be perfect and complete, needing nothing. James 1:2-4 (NLT)

Thought

Is patience the same as inaction?

Complacency does not demonstrate the Kingdom of God.

Patience is releasing your will, so God's will can be done through you. God's will has moments of sitting still – Jesus always spent time alone with God. When we choose to do the same… to discipline ourselves to sit still longer than fifteen minutes… we learn to move to the rhythms of His grace.

His rhythm seldom means inaction. Even when we wait on God, we must choose to wait with expectation. We know He's good and is the giver of good gifts. We know He won't give His children a stone when they ask for bread, or a serpent when they ask for a fish.

Patience becomes real when our timetables get set aside for God's timetable. If God wasn't patient with us – not wanting for any to perish – none of us would be here.

It's His patience with us that we need to reflect to the part of the world that is away from the Son.

How do we do that?

We show love. Remember, it's the antidote to negativity. Love is patient. It is kind. It reflects who God is – as do all the fruit of the Spirit we're growing in our lives.

Don't worry, if not today, soon, you will have an opportunity for your faith to be tested to produce even more patience. Today you'll need to choose to be patient with others, and so doing, show God's love to them.

Prayer

Lord, I know that You are patient with me and I know I haven't been patient with (insert the names). Thank You that You'll help me become more like You. Thank You that You're helping me to show Your love to others. I choose to be patient today and always. Help me to be patient to bring glory to You.

Challenge

Go the speed limit today. Stop at all red lights. Change your schedule so that you're not in a rush. Slow down and show patience for others.

Declaration

I choose to reflect the light of the Son to the side of the world that's away from the Son. I choose to put on love, joy, peace, patience, kindness, goodness, faithfulness, gentleness and self-control.

DAY 19

Reflection

I am kind to everyone in my every day world. I look out for their interests and not merely my own. I do nothing out of selfish ambition or vain conceit. I don't live to work or work to live. In humility, I consider others ahead of myself. I don't do what I do to get a reward or look good in the eyes of others. They see my good works and glorify my Father in heaven.

Reflection Question:

Have I been looking out for my own interests lately?

KINDNESS RULES

DEVOTIONAL

But I say, love your enemies! Pray for those who persecute you! In that way, you will be acting as true children of your Father in heaven. For he gives his sunlight to both the evil and the good, and he sends rain on the just and the unjust alike. If you love only those who love you, what reward is there for that? Even corrupt tax collectors do that much. If you are kind only to your friends, how are you different from anyone else? Even pagans do that. But you are to be perfect, even as your Father in heaven is perfect. Matthew 5:44-48 (NLT)

Thought

Can you remember the last time someone showed you kindness ...when it wasn't to repay something you did for him or her, or to sell you something, or even to make an impression?

Doesn't it just encourage you to remember someone like that?

Those are the people I like to hang around. They are the ones I need to learn from.

Of course, most have learned it from God. Did you know God enjoys showing kindness towards all He has made?

> ...but let him who boasts, boast about this:
> that he understands and knows me, that I am the LORD, who exercises kindness, justice and righteousness on earth, for in these I delight," declares the LORD. Jeremiah 9:24 (NIV)

Did you know there are results when we don't respond to His kindness?

> About that time Hezekiah became deathly ill. He prayed to the Lord, who healed him and gave him a miraculous sign. But Hezekiah did not respond appropriately to the kindness shown him, and he became proud. So the Lord's anger came against him and against Judah and Jerusalem. 2 Chronicles 32:24-25 (NLT)

Did you know God alone can respond the way He did against Hezekiah?

> Do not take revenge, my friends, but leave room for God's wrath, for it is written: "It is mine to avenge; I will repay," says the Lord. Romans 12:19 (NIV)

God's justice is for God alone to wield. Jesus wants us to leave everything in God's hands and to reflect the nature of God to those who can't pay us back.

> Then Jesus said to his host, "When you give a luncheon or dinner, do not invite your friends, your brothers or relatives, or your rich neighbors; if you do, they may invite you back and so you will be repaid. But when you give a banquet, invite the poor, the crippled, the lame, the blind, and you will be blessed. Although they cannot repay you, you will be repaid at the resurrection of the righteous." Luke 14:12-14 (NIV)

Can we be kind and expect nothing in return?

Can we obey what Jesus said in Luke 6:35 and show kindness to even those who consider us enemies?

You can because the nature of God is written and being rewritten on the parchment of your heart. You are shining

His light to the side of the world that's away from the Son. And He empowers you to do it:

1. Because of God

2. With Jesus

3. Empowered by the Holy Spirit

These are the Kindness Rules to allow kindness to rule.

Prayer

Lord, thank You for showing me kindness and help me to respond to it by showing it to others. I don't want this to be a program I try for a certain number of days. I need this to be the pattern for my life. Help me to show kindness to all – to those close, to those against, and to those who cannot repay. Show me who I can show Your kindness to today and how I can do it, so You get the glory.

Challenge

There's someone that has come to your mind that you need to be kind to today. It could be a neighbour, a co-worker, an extended family member, a person on the bus or a stranger on the street. Show them kindness that isn't owed them, and don't do it to have kindness returned. Send us your stories - http://revtrev.link/mystory

Declaration

I choose to reflect the light of the Son to the side of the world that's away from the Son. I choose to put on love, joy, peace, patience, kindness, goodness, faithfulness, gentleness and self-control.

DAY 20

Reflection

I do good to everyone in my everyday world. I choose to smile to put people at ease. I am friendly and find people are friendly back. I look for ways I can bless and not have it taken as a curse. I look out for the interests of others and not merely my own.

Reflection Question:

Have I been doing good to others lately?

IT'S GOOD TO DO GOOD

DEVOTIONAL

How can I repay the LORD for all his goodness to me? Psalm 116:12 (NIV)

Thought

I don't consider myself a modern thinker. I'm resistant to the labels others try to force on me. I think about webs of relationships, not linear cause-and-effect. I can hold multiple conflicting thoughts without any angst. And I'm a follower of Christ.

I know this makes some people nervous. However, I'm believing that from post-post-modernity the greatest theologians in history will emerge.

I do have a problem with the way many people, especially those with my thinking process, carry out truth. We can believe something is true, but it doesn't make a difference in our lives. Truth doesn't matter if we don't work out its implication in our lives. If it doesn't matter, can it be true?

Let me give you an example.

Ask anyone to create a scale of goodness. Pick a spot on the wall – the top is good, the bottom is bad. Tell them to choose an example for the bottom – it'll be someone like Hitler. Ask them to have an example for the top – Mother Teresa will usually come up. Ask them where they think the average person in the world is on the continuum and depending on their view of life, the average will be anywhere from the middle of the scale or slightly below, up to halfway or to the top or slightly more.

Now, ask them to say where they are. We inevitably say we're better than the average. (If you don't think you are, you may have some issues with guilt. Read 1 John 1:9, then repent and know you're forgiven.)

How can we all be better than average?

It is because we judge ourselves by our intent and judge everyone else by their actions.

Sorry news... the Bible tells us to judge goodness by what we do. Intentions are not good enough. It's not "being good' that is important, it's "doing good" that counts with God.

> Finally, all of you should be of one mind. Sympathize with each other. Love each other as brothers and sisters. Be tenderhearted, and keep a humble attitude. Don't repay evil for evil. Don't retaliate with insults when people insult you. Instead, pay them back with a blessing. That is what God has called you to do, and he will bless you for it. For the Scriptures say, "If you want to enjoy life and see many happy days, keep your tongue from speaking evil and your lips from telling lies. Turn away from evil and do good. Search for peace, and work to maintain it. The eyes of the Lord watch over those who do right, and his ears are open to their prayers. But the Lord turns his face against those who do evil." 1 Peter 3:8-13 (NLT)

So as we intentionally grow the fruit of goodness, we need to do "good". We don't need to feel "good". We don't need to think "good". We need to do "good".

And you already know what "good" is because you belong to the One who is Good.

> Do to others as you would have them do to you. Luke 6:31 (NIV)

Who will you show goodness to today?

Prayer

Lord, thank You for creating me the way I am. Thank You I was born for this time and created for eternity. Thank You so much for the goodness You've shown me. I am grateful for Your forgiveness and mercy and provision and blessing. Empower me, Holy Spirit, to show that same goodness to someone today.

Challenge

Treat everyone today, the way you would want to be treated. That includes the telemarketer that calls during supper and the unenlightened individual that cuts you off in traffic while he or she was talking on his or her mobile. Make it a habit... who knows where it could lead?

Declaration

I choose to reflect the light of the Son to the side of the world that's away from the Son. I choose to put on love, joy, peace, patience, kindness, goodness, faithfulness, gentleness and self-control.

DAY 21

REFLECTION

I am faithful in little things and have been entrusted with larger. I am intentional to keep the main thing the main thing. I love God and love people so that they can love God and love people. I worship Christ as Lord of my life and when anyone asks me about my hope as a believer, I am always ready to explain it and explain it in a gentle and respectful way.

Reflection Question:

Have I been ready and able to share my faith lately?

GODLY TENACITY OVER TIME

DEVOTIONAL

If you are faithful in little things, you will be faithful in large ones. But if you are dishonest in little things, you won't be honest with greater responsibilities. Luke 16:10 (NLT)

Thought

How long does it take for a mountain to rise from the sea? How long does it take for the rivers to take the stone back to the ocean depths? How long will it be before there is more usable beachfront on the Hawaiian Islands... and is it too early to invest?

Have you noticed how God thinks generationally? He's the God of Abraham, Isaac and Jacob. Yet we tend to think in terms of yesterday... and maybe tomorrow. No wonder faithfulness is such an obscure idea for many of our minds to grasp.

Faithfulness is Godly tenacity over time.

Should we dissect that a bit? "Godly" means it is in line or obedient to the will of God. "Tenacity" is simply stick-to-it-ness. And over time means it's not for a moment.

So can we define what God wants us to be faithful in? There are a few thoughts in scripture that focus on the need for our faithfulness.

Be True To Your Word

> Just say a simple, 'Yes, I will,' or 'No, I won't.' Anything beyond this is from the evil one. Matthew 5:37 (NLT)

Honour Your Marriage

> Give honour to marriage, and remain faithful to one another in marriage. God will surely judge people who are immoral and those who commit adultery. Hebrews 13:4 (NLT)

Use Your Talents

God has given each of you a gift from his great variety of spiritual gifts. Use them well to serve one another. 1 Peter 4:10 (NLT)

Guard Your Tongue

And the tongue is a flame of fire. It is a whole world of wickedness, corrupting your entire body. It can set your whole life on fire, for it is set on fire by hell itself. People can tame all kinds of animals, birds, reptiles, and fish, but no one can tame the tongue. It is restless and evil, full of deadly poison. Sometimes it praises our Lord and Father, and sometimes it curses those who have been made in the image of God. And so blessing and cursing come pouring out of the same mouth. Surely, my brothers and sisters, this is not right! James 3:6-10 (NLT)

Manage Your Money

> And if you are untrustworthy about worldly wealth, who will trust you with the true riches of heaven? Luke 16:11 (NLT)

Be Committed To Your Local Church

> Be devoted to one another in brotherly love. Honour one another above yourselves. Never be lacking in zeal, but keep your spiritual fervour, serving the Lord. Romans 12:10-11 (NIV)

We can't do these things for a season and consider ourselves to be faithful. You can't honour your marriage until times get tough. You can't use your talent until your interest wanes. You can't manage your money well just until there is a good sale.

You can't be a little bit pregnant and you can't be a little bit faithful. You either are or you are not.

The great news is God is faithful.

> If we are faithless, He remains faithful; for He cannot deny Himself. 2 Timothy 2:13 (NLT)

Because He's faithful, we can have faith in Him to finish what He's started.

> And I am certain that God, who began the good work within you, will continue his work until it is finally finished on the day when Christ Jesus returns. Philippians 1:6 (NLT)

So if today is the day you start having godly tenacity over time, then great. Welcome. None of us can ever say "I've arrived." But it's wonderful to have one more on the journey.

God is going to bless you for it:

> He grants a treasure of common sense to the honest. He is a shield to those who walk with integrity. He guards the paths of the just and protects those who are faithful to him. Proverbs 2:7-8 (NLT)

Prayer

Lord, I haven't always been faithful. I confess my sin and ask You to forgive me. Thank You that Your word says when I confess my sins, You are faithful and just to forgive me of those sins and to clean me from all unrighteousness. I want to be faithful because I want to reflect Your faithfulness to those who can only see You through me.

Challenge

Are you faithfully managing everything that God has entrusted to you? Is there one of the areas above that you are struggling in? Confess it to a friend and to God and ask them to hold you accountable to be faithful.

Declaration:

I choose to reflect the light of the Son to the side of the world that's away from the Son. I choose to put on love, joy, peace, patience, kindness, goodness, faithfulness, gentleness and self-control.

DAY 22

Reflection

In repentance and rest is my salvation. In quietness and trust is my strength. I govern my anger whenever I am provoked and patiently bear out the anger of others, even when it's been misplaced on me. My gentleness is evident to all. I trust God to fight my battles. I take up my position, stand firm and see the deliverance of the Lord.

Reflection Question:

How do I respond to anger lately?

Is Meekness Weakness?

Devotional

Let your gentleness be evident to all. The Lord is near.
Philippians 4:5 (NIV)

Thought

Mothers like to label their sons as "gentle." I've never seen a son respond well to that label. I somehow remember starting a fight with someone just to prove I wasn't "gentle." How's that for a fallen nature?

Gentleness is an expression of compassion seen as God deals with the frail and weak, and it's also His expectation for how His followers should treat one another. He is the sun, we are the moon. We reflect the light of the sun to the side of the world that's away from its direct glory.

We're told to be gentle with everyone:

> Remind the believers to submit to the government and its officers. They should be obedient, always ready to do what is good. They must not slander anyone and must avoid quarreling. Instead, they should be gentle and show true humility to everyone. Titus 3:1-2 (NLT)

But specifically we're to be gentle with others in the following circumstances:

Correcting The Wayward

> Dear brothers and sisters, if another believer is overcome by some sin, you who are godly should gently and humbly help that person back onto the right path. And be careful not to fall into the same temptation yourself. Galatians 6:1 (NLT)

> A servant of the Lord must not quarrel but must be kind to everyone, be able to teach, and be patient with difficult people. Gently instruct those who oppose the truth. Perhaps God will change

> those people's hearts, and they will learn the truth. 2 Timothy 2:24-25 (NLT)

Reasoning with pre-Christians

> Instead, you must worship Christ as Lord of your life. And if someone asks about your Christian hope, always be ready to explain it. But do this in a gentle and respectful way. Keep your conscience clear. Then if people speak against you, they will be ashamed when they see what a good life you live because you belong to Christ. 1 Peter 3:15-16 (NLT)

Nurturing the newly planted

> As apostles of Christ we could have been a burden to you, but we were gentle among you, like a mother caring for her little children. 1 Thessalonians 2:7 (NIV)

Jesus was meek, but He wasn't weak. He didn't need to exert His authority, He moved in His authority. We're to be like Christ in this world. We don't need to defend ourselves, we don't need to force others to see things the same way we do.

I absolutely enjoy how Eugene Peterson gets this sentiment across.

> Since this is the kind of life we have chosen, the life of the Spirit, let us make sure that we do not just hold it as an idea in our heads or a sentiment in our hearts, but work out its implications in every detail of our lives. That means we will not compare ourselves with each other as if one of us were better and another worse. We have far more interesting things to do with our lives. Each of us is an original. Live creatively, friends. Galatians 5:25-6:1a (The Message)

When you look to Christ, it's hard to judge someone else with anything but gentleness. We need to choose to be gentle.

Prayer

Lord, if I have shown disdain for gentleness, I confess it as sin and ask for Your forgiveness. Help me to be like Christ who would not break a bruised reed or snuff out a smouldering wick. Give me Your mind to know how to react in every situation. Empower me to be gentle to everyone.

Challenge

A soft answer turns away wrath. The next time you have an opportunity to be harsh, choose to be gentle.

Declaration

I choose to reflect the light of the Son to the side of the world that's away from the Son. I choose to put on love, joy, peace, patience, kindness, goodness, faithfulness, gentleness and self-control.

DAY 23

Reflection

I control my attitudes and actions. The same power that raised Christ from the dead lives in me. I've been given everything I need for life and godliness. Holy Spirit empowers me to accomplish every good work prompted by faith.
I am self-controlled and alert. I know the enemy prowls around like a roaring lion, but the God of peace has placed satan underneath my feet. I am forgiven and empowered to become more and more like Jesus.

Reflection Question:

Have I been self-controlled lately?

SAVOURING SELF-CONTROL

DEVOTIONAL

So think clearly and exercise self-control. Look forward to the gracious salvation that will come to you when Jesus Christ is revealed to the world. 1 Peter 1:13 (NLT)

Thought

Self-control is a mark of wisdom. Proverbs 29:11 says, "A fool gives full vent to his anger, but a wise man keeps himself under control" (NIV). Self-control is one of the most difficult fruit to grow for some people.

Our culture tells us to, "Buy now, pay later." We move out of our parent's home and want to get everything they took a lifetime to gather, in just a couple of years. We're taught to have an attention span of 6 minutes – until the next commercial. We're trained to expect instant gratification.

So is there any hope to grow the fruit of self-control?

With God, there is always hope. It's so much easier to be self-controlled when you let the Spirit control you.

Here's an example: I've tried different times to diet and lose some weight. I don't have the self-control to stick to it. But my wife and I felt led by God to do an extended Daniel fast. We abstained from everything but vegetables, fruit, water, whole grains and nuts. I was doing it in obedience to God and unto him. I knew it was His will and that He would help me do His will. I wasn't trying to lose weight, but I did.

So it's good to know His will and that He helps us to do His will.

It's His will for us to control our bodies:

> God's will is for you to be holy, so stay away from all sexual sin. Then each of you will control his own body and live in holiness and honour—not in lustful passion like the pagans who do not know God and his ways. Never harm or cheat a Christian brother in this matter by violating his wife, for the Lord avenges all such sins, as we have solemnly warned you before. God has called us to live holy lives, not impure lives. 1 Thessalonians 4:3-7 (NLT)

It's His will for us to control our minds:

> The end of all things is near. Therefore, be clear minded and self-controlled so that you can pray. 1 Peter 4:7 (NIV)

It's His will for us to control our mouths:

> Watch your tongue and keep your mouth shut, and you will stay out of trouble. Proverbs 21:23 (NLT)

And He's given us the Holy Spirit to teach and empower us to live self-controlled lives:

> For the grace of God that brings salvation has appeared to all men. It teaches us to say "No" to ungodliness and worldly passions, and to live self-controlled, upright and godly lives in this present age... Titus 2:11-12 (NIV)

Isn't God good?

Prayer

Lord, I need Your help to grow self-control. I know it's not my determination that makes me right before You. It's Your grace and mercy that I need to grow this fruit. Empower me to control my body, my thoughts and my mouth...all for Your glory.

Challenge

Do you need to grow self-control in an area of your life? Confess it to God, ask Him to help you, and then find someone today to help you stay accountable.

Declaration

I choose to reflect the light of the Son to the side of the world that's away from the Son. I choose to put on love, joy, peace, patience, kindness, goodness, faithfulness, gentleness and self-control.

STEP 4: THE REAL ME

DAY 24

Reflection

By the grace of God I am who I am. And His grace was not without effect. He has redeemed and called me His own. I am loved and have been bought with a price. He will finish the good work He's started in me. I don't mean to say that I have already achieved these things or that I have already reached perfection. But I press on to possess that perfection for which Christ Jesus first possessed me.

Reflection Question:

Have I been seeing myself from God's perspective lately?

REPLACING LIES WITH THE TRUTH

DEVOTIONAL

You will show me the way of life, granting me the joy of your presence and the pleasures of living with you forever. Psalm 16:11 (NLT)

Thought

We all have lies we choose to believe. These lies come in to help us "heal" wounds that we've been afflicted with. It's not actual healing that occurs; it's a snare of the enemy to gain a stronghold in our lives.

Try this exercise:

1. List 10 words of affirmation that have stuck with you since you first heard them.

2.

> Now list 10 words of death that have stuck with you since you first heard them.

Which list was easier to recall? Which list had more emotional triggers?

Living in a fallen world, and living with fallen people, we've all been wounded. Lies are what others have told us in our past. They may not have been spoken to us directly, but we've internalized them nonetheless. They are deceitful, downgrading and condemning.

For example:

"I can't do it."

"I'm worthless."

"I'm stupid."

"I'm ugly."

"I'm useless."

They are so much a part of us that until we can see the lies, we won't know we have them. We won't know how to see them, until we know who we are in Christ.

In Christ, there is now no more condemnation (Romans 8:1) so we know the thoughts that we are condemned with are not His.

The power of God can set you free from the chains of condemnation. This is your part to play:

> For though we live in the world, we do not wage war as the world does. The weapons we fight with are not the weapons of the world. On the contrary, they have divine power to demolish strongholds. We demolish arguments and every pretension that sets itself up against the knowledge of God, and we take captive every thought to make it obedient to Christ. 2 Corinthians 10:3-5 (NIV)

You heal the wounds the lies have sought to cover up by choosing to believe and live out of the truth. Over the next few chapters, we'll focus on four areas where many followers of Christ cling to lies. What we want to do is transform our thinking, so we won't be squeezed into the mould of the world.

> "Don't let the world around you squeeze you into its own mould, but let God remould your minds from within, so that you may prove in practice that the plan of God for you is good, meets all his demands, and moves toward the goal of true maturity" Romans 12:1-3 (Phillips)

We don't have time to cover all the areas where Christians may have strongholds in their thinking. But we don't want you to be unprepared.

Go to **http://revtrev.link/tips** and sign up for the **Tips and Tools to Fast from Negativity**. You're able to print off a personalized "Identity in Christ" as well as your name in the book of Ephesians. These are wonderful tools to help you know the truth about how God sees you. If you've already printed them off, have you been meditating and memorizing them? You can start that now.

Choose to replace the lies with the truth.

Prayer

Lord, show me the areas where I believe lies. Forgive me of them and remould my thinking with the truth of how You see me. I will fill my mind with Your thoughts and allow healing to take place in my wounded-ness. Amen.

Challenge

Go to **http://revtrev.link/tips** and sign up for the **Tips and Tools to Fast from Negativity** and print off your personalized "Identity in Christ". If you've done that already, pull them out and commit them to memory. Read the truths out loud. Pray them with authority; knowing it's how God sees you. You can also check out the **Live LIGHT Above the Negativity Course** and get help to take thought captive, tear down strongholds and demolish arguments that set themselves up against the knowledge of Christ. Get it for the best price with this link **http://revtrev.link/bless**

Declaration

I choose to believe what God says about me. I choose to live out of what I choose to believe. I choose to replace the lies that have attached themselves to wounds from my past with the truth of how God sees my situation and me.

DAY 25

Reflection

I am part of God's masterpiece. He has created me anew in Christ Jesus, so I can do the good things he planned for me long ago. Even before he made the world, God loved me and chose me in Christ to be holy and without fault in his eyes. God decided in advance to adopt me into his own family by bringing me to himself through Jesus Christ. This is what he wanted to do, and it gave him great pleasure. I belong to Christ and have become a new person. The old life is gone; a new life has begun! The Lord will work out his plans for my life.

Reflection Question:

Have I been acknowledging his favour on me lately?

I AM VALUABLE

DEVOTIONAL

But now, God's Message, the God who made you in the first place, Jacob, the One who got you started, Israel: "Don't be afraid, I've redeemed you. I've called your name. You're mine. When you're in over your head, I'll be there with you. When you're in rough waters, you will not go down. When you're between a rock and a hard place, it won't be a dead end— Because I am God, your personal God, The Holy of Israel, your Savior. I paid a huge price for you... Isaiah 43:1-2 (The Message)

Thought

How many times have you heard someone mutter "worthless" under his or her breath? If you listen closely, sometimes you hear "I'm" before "worthless". Do you ever catch yourself saying something similar -"Loser", "Stupid", "Nobody"?

Stop it.

While it's tough to change that thinking on your own, you can renew your mind by the word of God. The Holy Spirit can quicken the thoughts of God for you. He can make them come alive and change you from the inside out.

Although there are many solid Christians reading this right now, I know we are all connected to people who need to live the truth of how God sees them. So I'm just going to point you to **http://revtrev.link/tips** and sign up for the **Tips and Tools to Fast from Negativity**. We have a tool to help everyone personalize his or her identity in Christ. Fill in your name – or the name of your kids – or the name of someone you are going to email to encourage. Press the button and print off your personalized Identity in Christ.

I did the following for my daughter Taiessa. This is just the first part, because today we need to know that in Christ, you are valuable.

Taya Is Valuable.

John 1:12 **Taya is God's daughter.**
But Taya received Him, and to Taya He gave the right to become God's daughter, because Taya believes in His name.

John 15:5 **Taya is a part of the true vine, and a channel of Christ's life.**
I am the vine. Taya is a branch. If Taya remains in Me, and I in her, she will bear much fruit, for apart from Me, Taya can do nothing.

John 15:15 **Taya is a friend of Christ.**
No longer do I call Taya a servant, for a servant doesn't know what her lord does. But I have called Taya a friend, for everything that I heard from My Father, I have made known to Taya.

Rom. 8:17 **Taya is a joint heir with Christ, she shares Christ's inheritance with Him.**
And if a daughter, then an heir; an heir of God, and a joint-heir with Christ; if indeed Taya suffers with Him, that Taya may also be glorified with Him.

I Cor. 3:9 **Taya is God's co-worker.**
For Taya is one of God's fellow workers. Taya is God's field, God's building.

I Cor. 3:16 **Taya is God's temple.**
Don't you know that Taya is a temple of God, and that God's Spirit lives in her?

Eph. 1:5-6 **Taya has been adopted by God as His daughter.**
Having predestined Taya for adoption as a daughter through Jesus Christ to Himself, according to the good pleasure of His desire, to the praise of the glory of His grace, by which He freely bestowed favor on Taya in the Beloved.

Eph. 1:11 **Taya has an inheritance in Christ.**
In Him also Taya was assigned an inheritance, having been predestined according to the purpose of Him who works all things after the counsel of His will.

Eph. 2:5-6 **Taya has been made alive with Christ and she is seated with Christ in the heavenly places.**
Even when Taya was dead in her trespasses, God made her alive together with Christ (by grace Taya has been saved), and raised Taya up with Him and made Taya to sit with Him in the heavenly places in Christ Jesus.

Eph. 2:10 **Taya is God's workmanship, His handiwork.**
For Taya is His workmanship, created in Christ Jesus for good works, which God prepared before that Taya should walk in them.

Col. 1:27 **Christ Himself is in Taya.**
To whom God was pleased to make known what are the riches of the glory of this mystery among the Gentiles, which is Christ in Taya, the hope of glory.

Col. 3:3 **Taya 's life is hidden with Christ in God.**
For Taya died, and her life is hidden with Christ in God.

Taiessa is valuable because God places His value on her, and so are you, because He does the same for you.

Prayer

Lord, forgive me for repeating the words of death spoken over my life. Thank You for the words of life that flow from You. Thank You for calling me valuable – for calling me a child, a friend, an inheritor, a co-worker, and Your workmanship. Thank you, Lord, for not making any junk. Amen.

Challenge

Speak these words of life over yourself today. If you have an accountability partner, speak them over him or her as well. The words of life come from Christ. We need to speak the same.

Declaration

I choose to believe what God says about me. I choose to live out of what I choose to believe. I choose to replace the lies that have attached themselves to wounds from my past with the truth of how God sees my situation and me.

DAY 26

Reflection

I am loved with an everlasting love. He rejoices over me with singing. Since he is for me and not against me, who can be against me? He demonstrates his love in this, while I was still a sinner Christ died for me. He made the way so I can be with him in this life and for eternity. His banner over me is love. I am loved.

Reflection Question:

Have I felt loved lately?

I Am Loved

Devotional

O LORD, God of heaven, the great and awesome God, who keeps his covenant of love with those who love him and obey his commands. Nehemiah 1:5 (NIV)

Thought

Most people never see this in me because I'm socially bold, but I am really rather shy. I get my energy from ideas, not people. I don't "need" people to be around. I'm an ENFP. Most people don't get us. We're the most introverted extroverts. We get our energy from ideas, not people. Some groups of people have amazing ideas, and we get energy. Others have terrible ones and it drains us. I can be introverted in a crowd.

But if you're the least bit introverted, you may find all the "one another" commands a little overwhelming... here are just a few:

Be devoted to one another in brotherly love. Honour one another above yourselves. Romans 12:10 (NIV) **Live in harmony with one another**. Do not be proud, but be willing to associate with people of low position. Do not be conceited. Romans 12:16 (NIV) Therefore let us **stop passing judgment on one another**. Instead, make up your mind not to put any stumbling block or obstacle in your brother's or sister's way. Romans 14:13 (NIV) **Accept one another**, then, just as Christ accepted you, in order to bring praise to God. Romans 15:7 (NIV) I appeal to you, in the name of our Lord Jesus Christ, that all of you **agree with one another** so that there may be no divisions among you and that you may be perfectly united in mind and thought. 1 Corinthians 1:10 (NIV) You, my brothers, were called to be free. But do not use your freedom to indulge the sinful nature; rather, **serve one another in love.** Galatians 5:13 (NIV) **Be kind and compassionate to one another,** forgiving each other, just as in Christ God forgave you. Ephesians 4:32 (NIV) Be completely humble and gentle; be patient, **bearing with one another in love**. Ephesians 4:2 (NIV) **Submit to one another** out of reverence for Christ. Ephesians 5:21 (NIV) **Bear with each other** and forgive whatever grievances you may have against one another. Forgive as the Lord forgave you. Colossians 3:13 (NIV) Therefore **encourage one another and build each other up**, just as in fact you are doing. 1 Thessalonians 5:11 (NIV) But **encourage one another daily**, as long as it is called Today, so that none of you may be hardened by sin's deceitfulness. Hebrews 3:13 (NIV) And let us consider how we may **spur one another on toward love and good deeds**. Hebrews 10:24 (NIV) Let us not give up meeting together, as some are in the habit of doing, but let us **encourage one another**—and all the more as you see the Day approaching. Hebrews 10:25 (NIV) Now that you have purified yourselves by obeying the truth so that you have sincere love for your brothers, **love one another deeply**, from the heart. 1 Peter 1:22 (NIV) Finally, all of you, **live in harmony with one another**; be sympathetic, love as brothers, be compassionate and humble. 1 Peter 3:8 (NIV) Young men, in the same way, be submissive to those who are older. All of you, **clothe yourselves with humility toward one another**, because, "God opposes the proud but gives grace to the humble." 1 Peter 5:5 (NIV)

I could be intimidated by that list too, but I've learned a secret so that it's not difficult for me to fulfill these commands.

I've found that **when I'm a friend with someone, I naturally do all of these things.**

I have patience for them, I rejoice with them, I cry with them, I encourage them, I forgive them, I give way to them, I honour them and I look out for their interests. My secret is to make friends.

And I make friends knowing I can show them love, because God has shown love to me.

> Dear friends, since God so loved us, we also ought to love one another. 1 John 4:11 (NIV)

Because God loves us, we can show love that's sincere to others.

Aren't you convinced that you're loved? If you've printed off your personalized Identity in Christ, then read it to yourself and study the verses until you're convinced. If you haven't printed it off, go to **http://revtrev.link/tips**, sign up for **Tips and Tools to Fast from Negativity** and print it off right now.

Paul prayed for you when he prayed for the church in Ephesus:

> And I pray that you, being rooted and established in love, may have power, together with all the saints, to grasp how wide and long and high and deep is the love of Christ, and to know this love that surpasses knowledge—that you may be filled to the measure of all the fullness of God.
> Ephesians 3:17-19 (NIV)

If you don't believe it, make sure to print off the personalized book of Ephesians when you're at the site.

You are loved! Be filled with God's love!

Prayer

Oh Lord, that I would know the width and height and depth of Your love for me, so that I may experience this love that surpasses understanding. Lord, let Your love surround and encompass me so that it overflows from me to all You've placed in my web of relationships. Amen.

Challenge

Do you feel like a really big challenge today? Memorize your personalized Identity in Christ. Repeat the "I am Loved" portion out loud until you can say it in your sleep.

Declaration

I choose to believe what God says about me. I choose to live out of what I choose to believe. I choose to replace the lies that have attached themselves to wounds from my past with the truth of how God sees my situation and me.

DAY 27

Reflection

I am set free and called to freedom. I use my freedom to serve others in love. Since God is for me, who can be against me? Since he did not spare even his own Son but gave him up for me, won't he also give me everything else? Who can accuse? Who can condemn? He fights my battle. He is the mighty warrior. I walk in his victory.

Reflection Question:

Have I been walking in his victory lately?

I Am Victorious

Devotional

Can anything ever separate us from Christ's love? Does it mean he no longer loves us if we have trouble or calamity, or are persecuted, or hungry, or destitute, or in danger, or threatened with death? As the Scriptures say, "For your sake we are killed every day; we are being slaughtered like sheep." No, despite all these things, overwhelming victory is ours through Christ, who loved us. Romans 8:35-37 (NLT)

Thought

Why is a clock that is five minutes late more dangerous than one that is five hours early?

Because we pick up on lies that are way off, but the ones that seem to be truth we can more easily trust.

What did satan do when he tempted Christ in the desert? He used the truth about Jesus' situation and the partial truth from the word of God to tempt Christ into believing his version of the truth.

And he uses the same tactic with us today.

How often do we live as if we believe "the overwhelming victory is ours through Christ?" Be honest. It's usually the trouble or calamity, or persecution, or hunger, or destitution, or danger, or threats of death that really grab our attention.

It's time we replace those lies with the truth. I've used my son Kian as an example, but if you haven't done it yet, go to http://revtrev.link/tips and sign up for the **Tips and Tools to Fast from Negativity** and print off your own personalized Identity in Christ. It is so critical we live out of how God sees us. This is simply a tool to get it into your thinking.

Kian Is Victorious.

John 8:31-32 **Kian has been set free.**
If Kian remains in My word, then he is truly My disciple. Kian will know the truth, and the truth will make him free.

Rom. 6:1-4 **Kian died with Christ and he died to the power of sin's rule over his life.**
What shall we say then? Shall Kian continue in sin, that grace may abound? May it never be! If Kian died to sin, how could he live in it any longer? Or don't you know that when Kian was baptized into Christ Jesus, he was baptized into His death? Kian was buried with Him through baptism to death, that just

as Christ was raised from the dead through the glory of the Father, so Kian also might walk in newness of life.

Rom. 8:37 **Kian is more than a conqueror in Christ.**
No, in all these things, Kian is more than a conqueror through Him who loved him.

II Cor. 2:14 **Kian is led triumphantly by Christ.**
But thanks be to God, who always leads Kian in triumph in Christ, and reveals through Kian the sweet aroma of His knowledge in every place.

Gal. 2:20 **Kian was crucified with Christ.**
Kian has been crucified with Christ, and it is no longer Kian who lives, but Christ living in him. That life which Kian now lives in the flesh, he lives by faith in the Son of God, who loved Kian, and gave Himself up for him.

Phil. 4:13 **Kian can do all things through Christ.**
Kian can do all things through Christ, who strengthens him.

II Tim. 1:7 **Kian has been given a spirit of power, love and self-discipline.**
For God didn't give Kian a spirit of fear, but of power and love and self-discipline.

I John 5:4-5 **Kian has overcome the world.**
For Kian is born of God and overcomes the world. This is the victory that has overcome the world: Kian's faith. Kian overcomes the world because he believes that Jesus is the Son of God.

What is true with Kian is true for you. When your circumstance – even though it can be through no fault of your own - is contrary to the will of God expressed in Scripture, are you going to believe the Bible or your circumstance?

Having Jesus as your Lord means He's in the driver's seat of your life. It means when my life doesn't line up with Scripture, I change my life to agree with God. I can't ignore truth that He's revealed and I can't say it doesn't apply to me.

You are victorious. Believe it and live it!

Prayer

Lord, forgive me for looking at my circumstance instead of trusting in Your truth. When life in a fallen world happens, I haven't always run to You as I should have. I know Your plans for me are good because You are good. I know Your plans are to prosper me and not to harm me and to give me a hope and a future. I know that in Christ I am more than a conqueror and I choose to praise You in the storm. Amen.

Challenge

Take the verses listed under the "Kian is Victorious" section, look them up and meditate on them. Think about how much God loves you, despite your circumstance and praise Him before the answer comes.

Declaration

I choose to believe what God says about me. I choose to live out of what I choose to believe. I choose to replace the lies that have attached themselves to wounds from my past with the truth of how God sees my situation and me.

DAY 28

Reflection

I am chosen. God loves me and has chosen me to be part of his own people. I have received Holy Spirit, and he lives within me, so I don't need anyone to teach me what is true. For the Spirit teaches me everything I need to know. He guides me into all truth. The Creator of all is with me, goes before, comes behind and is inside me! How humbling and awesome that is to consider.

Reflection Question:

How has being chosen impacted my everyday life lately?

I AM CHOSEN

DEVOTIONAL

Even before he made the world, God loved us and chose us in Christ to be holy and without fault in his eyes. Ephesians 1:4 (NLT)

Thought

I am not my own. I have been bought with a price. I belong to God. I have been chosen before the foundation of the world. I have been set apart and called holy. I am His." These are words I often find coming from my lips to remind myself and satan whose I am. They just bubble up to encourage me.

I have had the experience of hearing the audible voice of God set me apart, and it absolutely wrecked my life. I can only explain it as feeling so insignificant and yet so highly valued that the only response left to me was unadulterated awe.

Sixteen years later, I know it wasn't just for a moment in time. We are receiving a kingdom that cannot be shaken, so we need to worship Him acceptably with all reverence and awe, because our God is a consuming fire (Hebrews 12:28-29).

So why do we relate to Him only as a friend?

Being chosen by a friend, really isn't that significant. Being chosen by the one who spoke the 400 million stars in this galaxy and the 400 million galaxies in this universe and potentially unlimited universes into being is highly significant.

It is for me... and it needs to be for you.

You are chosen, set apart, taught, loved and empowered by the Great I AM, the ever-living Father, the Alpha and Omega, the First and the Last - GOD.

How life-wrecking is that?

Oh, that you may have the spirit of wisdom and revelation that you may know the hope to which you have been called, the glorious inheritance in the saints and the incomparably great power for all who believe.

A friend sent this to me in an email. I usually don't pass them along, but this one caught my eye. Why do you think it's shaped like a bell? I think it's because we all need a wake-up call to our true identity in Christ.

I KNOW WHO I AM
I am God's child (John 1:12)
I am Christ's friend (John 15:15)
I am united with the Lord(1 Cor. 6:17)
I am bought with a price(1 Cor. 6:19-20)
I am a saint (set apart for God). (Eph. 1:1)
I am a personal witness of Christ (Acts 1:8)
I am the salt & light of the earth (Matt.5:13-14)
I am a member of the body of Christ(1 Cor 12:27)
I am free forever from condemnation (Rom. 8: 1-2)
I am a citizen of Heaven. I am significant (Phil.3:20)
I am free from any charge against me (Rom. 8:31-34)
I am a minister of reconciliation for God(2 Cor.5:17-21)
I have access to God through the Holy Spirit (Eph. 2:18)
I am seated with Christ in the heavenly realms (Eph. 2:6)
I cannot be separated from the love of God(Rom.8:35-39)
I am established, anointed, sealed by God (2 Cor.1:21-22)
I am assured all things work together for good (Rom. 8: 28)
I have been chosen and appointed to bear fruit (John 15:16)
I may approach God with freedom and confidence (Eph. 3: 12)
I can do all things through Christ who strengthens me (Phil. 4:13)
I am the branch of the true vine, a channel of His life (John 15: 1-5)
I am God's temple (1 Cor. 3: 16). I am complete in Christ (Col. 2: 10)
I am hidden with Christ in God (Col. 3:3). I have been justified (Romans 5:1)
I am God's co-worker (1 Cor. 3:9; 2 Cor 6:1). I am God's workmanship(Eph. 2:10)
I am confident that the good works God has begun in me will be perfected (Phil. 1: 5)
I have been redeemed and forgiven (Col. 1:14). I have been adopted as God's child(Eph 1:5)
I belong to God
Do you know
who you are!?

You're chosen. The accuser can't touch you. Know who you are in Christ and live out of that revelation today.

Prayer

Eternal Father, grant me the spirit of wisdom and revelation so that I will know the hope to which I have been called, the glorious inheritance in the saints and the incomparably great power for all who believe. I am Yours. I have been bought with a price. I belong to You. I have been chosen before the foundation of the world. Amen.

Challenge

Go over all the truths in the personalized Identity in Christ you printed off from signing up for the **Tips and Tools to Fast from Negativity** at **http://revtrev.link/tips** We didn't have time to cover them all directly, but other the next few days we'll be covering some of them from another angle. They are truth and truth is life so read them, pray them, declare them, pronounce them, know them, and live out of them.

Declaration

I choose to believe what God says about me. I choose to live out of what I choose to believe. I choose to replace the lies that have attached themselves to wounds from my past with the truth of how God sees my situation and me.

STEP 5: FORGIVENESS IS KEY

DAY 29

Reflection

I have confessed my sin and I am forgiven. The enemy can't condemn me, so I can't condemn myself. I have done what I can to make amends to all I that I can. I've sought forgiveness from others and also my Father. As far as it depends on me, I live in peace with all people. I am free from all condemnation.

Reflection Question:

Have I been keeping accounts short with God and people lately?

God Has Forgiven Me

Devotional

If we say we have no sin [refusing to admit that we are sinners], we delude and lead ourselves astray, and the Truth [which the Gospel presents] is not in us [does not dwell in our hearts]. If we [freely] admit that we have sinned and confess our sins, He is faithful and just (true to His own nature and promises) and will forgive our sins [dismiss our lawlessness] and [continuously] cleanse us from all unrighteousness [everything not in conformity to His will in purpose, thought, and action]. If we say (claim) we have not sinned, we contradict His Word and make Him out to be false and a liar, and His Word is not in us [the divine message of the Gospel is not in our hearts]. 1 John 1:8-10 (AMP)

Thought

Are you a follower of Christ who struggles with having a victorious daily walk with the Lord?

If so, it may be because of the sin of un-forgiveness. God cannot violate his perfect nature and overlook our sin. Un-forgiveness is a common stronghold the devil has in the lives of many of God's children. We believe lies about forgiveness and live according to those lies.

You do not need to be perfect before Christ forgives you and welcomes you into His kingdom. He loves you the way you are... and wants to empower you to forgive others, to be forgiven by others, and to accept the forgiveness He freely offers you.

You can arrive at this by first admitting you've fallen short of the impossible standard of a Perfect God... you're not perfect.

We're all ready to admit that, but most of us use it as an excuse not to do better and don't understand what that means to the reality of life.

When we say, "I'm only human," it's only true in the sense that we're only fallen humans. We are not what we were created to be.

> When Adam sinned, sin entered the entire human race. Adam's sin brought death, so death spread to everyone, for everyone sinned. Romans 5:12 (NLT)

We were created to be in close relationship with our Creator. We were created to not be separated from God, His creation, our partners, and ourselves and yet this is our reality.

Since sin came into the world, we have been separated from our true identities. We are separated from others and separated from creation. Perhaps most importantly, we are separated from the one who created us and saw every one of our days before one of them came to be.

But that changes when you admit you've fallen short... admit that you've sinned. The Bible says when we confess our sins; God will forgive us and cleanse us.

> If we claim to be without sin, we deceive ourselves and the truth is not in us. If we confess our sins, he is faithful and just and will forgive us our sins and purify us from all unrighteousness. If we claim we have not sinned, we make him out to be a liar and his word has no place in our lives. 1 John 1:8-10 (NIV)

This is what happens when you tell God you're sorry and decide to live your life with the knowledge that Jesus is in the driver's seat of your life.

When your life doesn't line up with Scripture, you change your life so that it does. You don't ignore what the Bible says or complain, "It's too difficult." If God wants you to do something, He'll empower you to do it.

Now some of you are saying, "I already knew all that."

Great. Maybe you need to share it with someone else today?

But I want you to ask yourself, "Have I worked out its implication in every area of my life?"

If you have started, then God can empower you to do the difficult things we are going to discuss over the next few days. They are part of His will, so He'll help you to do them.

Prayer

Lord, Thank you for Your forgiveness. Thank You that as I confess my sins to You, You are faithful and just to forgive me my sins and to cleanse me from all unrighteousness. Thank You, Holy Spirit, that You empower me to do the will of God. Thank You for preparing me for a deeper walk with You. Amen.

Challenge

Thank God for forgiving you of your confessed sins. Thank Him for forgiving the ones you remember. Thank Him for forgiving the ones that you've since forgot. Ask God if you need to forgive someone else.

Declaration

I choose to forgive everyone who has wronged me. I choose to seek the forgiveness of those I have wronged. I choose to accept I have been forgiven of my confessed sin. I choose to walk in the freedom forgiveness brings.

DAY 30

Reflection

I forgive as God forgave me. Before I deserved it, he made the way for me to friends again with him. I didn't have to change before I could be changed. I forgive others for my sake and not just their sake. I forgive freely, and allow trust to be re-earned. I've been forgiven so much, I have to forgive with my whole heart. Holy Spirit enables me to do this, even when I've been hurt.

Reflection Question:

Have I been holding on to unforgiveness lately?

FORGIVENESS CONFUSION

Devotional

Bear with each other and forgive whatever grievances you may have against one another. Forgive as the Lord forgave you.
Colossians 3:13 (NIV)

Thought

Too many followers of Christ are confused about forgiveness. They live out of lies they hold to as truth. We'll be looking at some of those lies today.

We don't forgive because we believe the violator needs to pay. We feel the one who did us wrong needs to understand what we were put through. We want the one who sinned to acknowledge what they did and make amends.

But we must awaken to the fact that un-forgiveness leads to bitterness and separation from God. He has forgiven us and wants to enable us to make the choice to forgive those who have sinned against us.

Here are some questions I've come across over the years. If someone else has asked them, I know other people are thinking them. Let's use Scripture to clear up the confusion.

Q. Does the offender pay if I don't forgive?

A. No. But you pay. You only harm yourself when you refuse to forgive wrongs done to you.

> For if you forgive others their trespasses, your heavenly Father will also forgive you; but if you do not forgive others, neither will your Father forgive your trespasses. (Matthew 6:14-15 NRSV)

> If you forgive others, you will be forgiven. (Luke 6:37 NLT)

Un-forgiveness is a sin God cannot look upon. It separates us from our loving Creator. If you want to see how serious it is, check out Jesus' parable of the unrepentant servant in Matthew 18:21-35.

Q. Does forgiving someone let him or her "off the hook"?

A. No. It puts them into God's hands.

> Do not take revenge, my friends, but leave room for God's wrath, for it is written: "It is mine to avenge; I will repay," says the Lord. Romans 12:19 (NIV)

Q. Shouldn't I wait until they change before I forgive?

A. No.

> Forgive as Christ forgave you. Colossians 3:13 (NIV)

How is that?

> While we were still sinners, Christ died for us. Romans 5:8 (NIV)

Before we deserved it... He showed us grace. You must choose to forgive whoever has wronged you. We forgive for the sake of our relationship with God, not for the sake of the other person.

Q. But Christ doesn't forgive me until I ask for it, so shouldn't I wait to forgive someone until they ask for it?

A. No. First, you aren't God. You don't have His capacity for grace. Second, understand that you forgive for your sake, not theirs. Christ said in Matthew 18 that if we don't forgive another from our hearts, tormentors will be assigned to us. If you don't forgive someone until they ask for forgiveness, you're actually letting them keep you imprisoned.

Q. Shouldn't I wait until I feel like forgiving?

A. We are told to forgive with our whole heart. The Hebrew understanding of the heart is that yes, it is the seat of our emotions, but it's also the seat of our decision AND the seat of our action. We can decide to forgive and we can choose to bless. Sometimes peace comes to us and we feel like we've forgiven. IF we don't feel like we've forgiven, God wants to heal the lie we're believing. You can feel like you've forgiven...but don't wait to feel like you can forgive. Contact me if you need help with this.

> Make allowance for each other's faults, and forgive anyone who offends you. Remember, the Lord forgave you, so you must forgive others.
> Colossians 3:13 (NLT)

Q. Do I need to trust someone I forgive?

A. No. Forgiveness and trust are two separate issues.

Forgiveness is given while trust is earned. Forgiving someone does not mean they don't face the consequences for their actions. It does not mean you put yourself into harm's way. You are not a doormat for those who would hurt you.

Now you may have other misconceptions about forgiveness, and we may cover some in the next couple of days. But many followers of Christ stumble on these points. So even if you're not struggling with forgiving someone, you are close to someone who is. Help them to find the freedom of forgiveness.

Prayer

In the name of Jesus, I purpose and choose to forgive (the person) from my heart for (what they did). I acknowledge the hurt and the hate it has led to in my life and I agree to live with the consequences of their sin.

In the name of Jesus I cancel all the debts and obligations to me. I release (the person) to You, as well as my right to avenge.

Dear Lord, I ask You to forgive me for my bitterness toward (the person) in this situation. In the name of Jesus and in the power of His blood, I cancel satan's power over me in this memory because I have forgiven and have been forgiven by God.

In the name of Jesus, I command that all the tormentors that have been assigned to me because of my un-forgiveness leave me now.

Holy Spirit, I invite You into my heart and to heal me from this pain. Please speak Your words of truth to me about this situation.

This I pray in the name of Jesus Christ my Lord. Amen

Challenge

Ask God to reveal to you anyone that you may need to forgive. As you wait on Him, you may be surprised at who He brings to your mind. Choose to forgive them and release them into God's hands.

Declaration

I choose to forgive everyone who has wronged me. I choose to seek the forgiveness of those I have wronged. I choose to accept I have been forgiven of my confessed sin. I choose to walk in the freedom forgiveness brings.

DAY 31

Reflection

I forgive with my whole heart. I decide to forgive. It's a decision of my will. I act like I've forgiven and bless those who have cursed me. I feel like I've forgiven and expose lies I believe to the truth he reveals when I don't. I know the freedom of forgiveness when I forgive with my whole heart.

Reflection Question:

Is there anyone I don't feel like I've forgiven?

When You Don't Feel Like You've Forgiven

Devotional

I have thought deeply about all that goes on here under the sun, where people have the power to hurt each other. I have seen wicked people buried with honor. Yet they were the very ones who frequented the Temple and are now praised in the same city where they committed their crimes! This, too, is meaningless. When a crime is not punished quickly, people feel it is safe to do wrong. But even though a person sins a hundred times and still lives a long time, I know that those who fear God will be better off. Ecclesiastes 8:9-12 (NLT)

Thought

Another lie we believe about forgiveness is that "If I can't forget, then I haven't forgiven." Don't you love it when people quote adages like they're Scripture? "Forgive and forget" has done so much damage to people's understanding of God and their relationship with others.

Do you realize God does not forget the sins He forgives us of? How could He and still be an all-knowing God? Instead, He chooses to not remember and hold them against us.

> "For I will forgive their wickedness and will remember their sins no more." Jeremiah 31:34 (NIV)

> Then he adds: "Their sins and lawless acts I will remember no more." Hebrews 10:17 (NIV)

This is more than just an exercise in semantics. We also can't easily forget. God has created us with minds to remember. Thoughts will pop back into our minds and we have no power over the past...but we do have control over how we let our past control our present and our future.

We need to forgive with our whole heart.

Your heart is the seat of your decision , the seat of your action AND the seat of your emotion.

So **forgiveness is a decision**, it's a choice. You decide to forgive.

And sometimes that's all you need. For start acting and feeling that you've forgiven.

Other times, you need to do more than just decide to forgive. You need to put an action to it. **forgiveness is an action**. Sometimes that's as simple as blessing the one who did you wrong.

Jesus taught his disciples:

> ""'But I say to you who listen: Love your enemies, do what is good to those who hate you, bless those who curse you, pray for those who mistreat you. If anyone hits you on the cheek, offer the other also. And if anyone takes away your coat, don't hold back your shirt either. Give to everyone who asks you, and from one who takes your things, don't ask for them back. Just as you want others to do for you, do the same for them. If you love those who love you, what credit is that to you? Even sinners love those who love them. If you do what is good to those who are good to you, what credit is that to you? Even sinners do that.

> And if you lend to those from whom you expect to receive, what credit is that to you? Even sinners lend to sinners to be repaid in full. But love your enemies, do what is good, and lend, expecting nothing in return. Then your reward will be great, and you will be sons of the Most High. For He is gracious to the ungrateful and evil. Be merciful, just as your Father also is merciful." Luke 6:27-36 (HCSB)

Paul teaches us:

> "If possible, on your part, live at peace with everyone. Friends, do not avenge yourselves; instead, leave room for His wrath. For it is written: Vengeance belongs to Me; I will repay, says the Lord. But If your enemy is hungry, feed him. If he is thirsty, give him something to drink. For in so doing you will be heaping fiery coals on his head. Do not be conquered by evil, but conquer evil with good." Romans 12:18-21 (HCSB)

So a blessing is an action that shows forgiveness.

Forgiveness is also an emotion.

Sometimes, when you to decide to forgive and then show that you've forgiven by blessing the person that did you wrong, your feelings fall into line and you begin to feel that you've forgiven.

Other times, feeling you've forgiven is next to impossible.

But God is God of the impossible and Jesus wouldn't have told us to forgive from the heart if it wasn't possible.

You need to **follow those feelings of unforgiveness.**

What would happen if you chose to forgive? What lie are you believing? Why are you believing that lie. Ask Jesus to show you when that lie became embedded in your understanding. Let him show you the truth of what happened.

This is how you put off bitterness. You learn to forgive others with your whole heart. Use the GRACE Tool.

The GRACE Tool

G - Get in touch with the emotion

R - Remember when you felt like this before

A - Accept what the feeling reveals

C - Centre in on the truth

E - Examine if the feelings have changed

G - Get in touch with the emotion

How does it make me feel? What comes to mind when I focus on what I'm feeling? When have I felt this way before?

R - Remember when you felt like this before

Is there an earlier emotion? How does that make me feel? Why do I feel that way? Why does believing _______ make me feel _____?

A - Accept what the feeling reveals

Not that it's true, but does it feel true that _____?

C - Centre in on the truth

What does God say about what I believe?

Lord, what do you want me to know?

E - Examine if the feelings have changed

Does it still feel true that ______?

Does it feel like I've forgiven the offence against me?

Why not pause now and invite Holy Spirit to do some work? Maybe you see the symptoms but don't know the cause. You feel bitterness, and you know you need to put it off. Ask Jesus if there's someone you need to forgive.

Did someone come to mind?

Will you make the choice to forgive?

Will you choose to bless them in word and, where possible, in deed?

Will you ask Holy Spirit to speak truth to your pain?

Prayer

Father, I acknowledge that I've held resentment and bitterness against ____________. I confess this as sin and ask you to forgive me. I forgive ______________. Remind me, Lord, to not hold any more resentments, but rather to love this person. Father, I ask you to also forgive __________________. Thank you for hearing and answering my prayer. In Jesus' name, Amen.

Challenge

If this truth was for you today, then apply it to your life. If remembering pain isn't your problem right now, be a light in a dark world and share this truth with someone who needs it today. Walk with them as they journey through the pain.

Declaration

I choose to forgive everyone who has wronged me. I choose to seek the forgiveness of those I have wronged. I choose to accept I have been forgiven of my confessed sin. I choose to walk in the freedom forgiveness brings.

DAY 32

REFLECTION

I humble myself towards others when I sin against them. It can be a sin of omission or a sin of commission. It can be a mistake, or it may be intentional. Hurt people hurt people, and I've been hurt by people and do hurt people. I don't excuse the pain I cause, I repent and make amends. I label what I've done or failed to do as wrong and acknowledge the hurt it has caused.

Reflection Question:

Is there anyone I need to ask forgiveness from?

When You Need Forgiveness

Devotional

...leave your sacrifice there at the altar. Go and be reconciled to that person. Then come and offer your sacrifice to God.
Matthew 5:24 (NLT)

Thought

We are fallen people living in a fallen world. That's not an excuse. We need to become more and more and more like Jesus. But there may be times when we have sinned against someone else and we need to make it right.

The rabbis taught that the sin against someone else was heavier than the sin against God, because God would always forgive, but someone else may not.

They didn't have the book of Romans, so Rabbi Paul had a different point of view we follow, but more about that in a bit. Jesus gave us a pattern to follow in Matthew 5:23-26:

> "So if you are presenting a sacrifice at the altar in the Temple and you suddenly remember that someone has something against you, leave your sacrifice there at the altar. Go and be reconciled to that person. Then come and offer your sacrifice to God. When you are on the way to court with your adversary, settle your differences quickly. Otherwise, your accuser may hand you over to the judge, who will hand you over to an officer, and you will be thrown into prison. And if that happens, you surely won't be free again until you have paid the last penny. (NLT)

There are a couple of things I'll point out right away. It's the one bringing the sacrifice that remembers someone has something against him or her. It's the Holy Spirit that brings it to their mind. It's the Spirit's job to convict sin, not any of ours. Jesus Christ didn't come into the world to condemn it, so how can we condemn a fellow believer (or the world for that matter)?

Neil T. Anderson gives the following advice in "The Steps to Freedom in Christ":

Only the actions, which have hurt another person, need to be confessed to them. If you have had jealous, lustful or angry thoughts toward another, and they don't know about it, these are to be confessed to God alone. An exception to this principle occurs when restitution needs to be made. If you stole or broke something, damaged someone's reputation, and so on, you need to go to that person and make it right, even if he or she is unaware of what you did.

The Process of Seeking Forgiveness

1. Write out what you did wrong and why you did it.

2. Make sure you have already forgiven the person for whatever he or she may have done to you.

3. Think through exactly how you will ask him or her to forgive you. Be sure to

- Label your action as wrong.
- Be specific and admit what you did.
- Make no defences or excuses.
- Do not blame the other person, and do not expect or demand that he or she asks for your forgiveness.

- Your confession should lead to the direct question: "Will you forgive me?"

4. Seek the right place and the right time to approach the offended person.

5. Ask for forgiveness in person from anyone with whom you can talk face-to-face with the following exception: Do not go alone when your safety might be in danger.

6. Except where no other means of communication is possible, do not write a letter because a letter can be very easily misread or misunderstood; a letter can be read by the wrong people (those having nothing to do with the offense or the confession); a letter can be kept when it should have been destroyed.

Now remember what I said about Rabbi Paul? Here's where his teaching comes in. Once you sincerely seek forgiveness, you are free-whether the other person forgives you or not. Paul wrote in Romans 12:18:

> Do all that you can to live in peace with everyone. (NLT)

So once you've sincerely sought forgiveness, you are free. So be sure to do what Jesus said in Matthew 5:24:

> ...leave your sacrifice there at the altar. Go and be reconciled to that person. Then come and offer your sacrifice to God. (NLT)

Asking forgiveness from someone we've wronged can be a very difficult thing to do. But now that you know the truth, remember the whole truth – God has not only told you to do it, He'll empower you to do it. It may be good to discuss these thoughts with your pastor if you need some support in doing what the Bible instructs you.

We're praying for you.

Prayer

Lord, thank You once again for forgiving me of all my sins. Thank You for cleansing me and making me a minister of reconciliation. If I have sinned against someone, I need to ask forgiveness from bring him or her to my memory and make it possible for me to seek reconciliation. Holy Spirit, help me do what pleases the Father. Amen.

Challenge

Is there someone you need to ask forgiveness from? Ask the Holy Spirit to remind you of anyone you may not be in the right relationship with. Wait in His presence and expect Him to speak. When images or thoughts go through your mind, confess them to God if you need to, and seek the forgiveness of others if you must.

Declaration

I choose to forgive everyone who has wronged me. I choose to seek the forgiveness of those I have wronged. I choose to accept I have been forgiven of my confessed sin. I choose to walk in the freedom forgiveness brings.

DAY 33

Reflection

I am set free and am free indeed! I strip off every weight that entangles and the sin that so easily trips me up. And I run with endurance the race God has set before me. I am under no condemnation in Christ. I have been saved by grace, through faith. It is a gift of God not a reward for anything I've done. I am free!

Reflection Question:

Have I been living free lately?

How to Feel That You Have Been Forgiven

Devotional

Jesus said to the people who believed in him, "You are truly my disciples if you remain faithful to my teachings. And you will know the truth, and the truth will set you free." John 8:31-33 (NLT)

Thought

There are many who, after being forgiven by God and after seeking the forgiveness of those they have offended, find it extremely difficult to live in the freedom that forgiveness brings.

Sometimes they don't feel they were worthy to be forgiven. This is true; all of us stand before God by His grace. But this is a liberating truth of scripture, not something that condemns us.

> Therefore, there is now no condemnation for those who are in Christ Jesus... Romans 8:1 (NIV)

But I've heard too many Christians teach that we need to forgive ourselves. I've actually heard it from my own lips. I've looked in Scripture and can't find forgiving ourselves in the book.

It's good psychology but lousy theology. It's justifying the sin of unbelief.

The word declares that

> But if we confess our sins to him, he is faithful and just to forgive us our sins and to cleanse us from all wickedness. 1 John 1:9 (NIV)

When you confess your sin, he's forgiven you, so who are you to hold a grudge?

You're not believing that you're forgiven.

The tools he's given us are confession and repentance. Confession means to agree with him that we're not believing we've been forgiven. We may not feel we're worthy. We may think we've done to much damage to receive His grace.

Repentance is changing our mind and going in the opposite direction. That can come by allowing the truth of the word to transform us.

> ...faith [comes] by hearing, and hearing by the word of God. Romans 10:17 (NKJV)

The following verses assure us that we are forgiven when we confess our sins. Remember - believe what the Bible says about you.

Read them.

Memorize them.

Meditate on them.

Confess and repent of the sin of unbelief.

Let them become alive to you. It's the living word of God that makes faith come alive. Pray them whenever you feel the condemning attack of satan saying you're not forgiven.

> If we claim to be without sin, we deceive ourselves and the truth is not in us. If we confess our sins, he is faithful and just and will forgive us our sins and purify us from all unrighteousness. 1 John 1:8-9 (NIV)

Cleanse me with hyssop, and I will be clean; wash me, and I will be whiter than snow. Psalms 51:7 (NIV)

...who forgives all your sins and heals all your diseases, who redeems your life from the pit and crowns you with love and compassion... Psalms 103:3-4 (NIV)

"Come now, let us reason together," says the LORD. "Though your sins are like scarlet, they shall be as white as snow; though they are red as crimson, they shall be like wool. Isaiah 1:18 (NIV)

Peter replied, "Repent and be baptized, every one of you, in the name of Jesus Christ for the forgiveness of your sins. And you will receive the gift of the Holy Spirit. Acts 2:38 (NIV)

Are any among you suffering? They should keep on praying about it. And those who have reason to be thankful should continually sing praises to the Lord. Are any among you sick? They should call

> for the elders of the church and have them pray over them, anointing them with oil in the name of the Lord. And their prayer offered in faith will heal the sick, and the Lord will make them well. And anyone who has committed sins will be forgiven. Confess your sins to each other and pray for each other so that you may be healed. The earnest prayer of a righteous person has great power and wonderful results. James 5:13-16 (NLT)

> My dear children, I write this to you so that you will not sin. But if anybody does sin, we have one who speaks to the Father in our defense—Jesus Christ, the Righteous One. He is the atoning sacrifice for our sins, and not only for ours but also for the sins of the whole world. 1 John 2:1-2 (NIV)

> People who cover over their sins will not prosper. But if they confess and forsake them, they will receive mercy. Proverbs 28:13 (NLT)

You are forgiven from sin that you confess and have done what you can to make right. Work these verses into your thinking if you need to, and pass the truth along to others you can encourage.

Prayer

Lord, show me Your love for me. Reveal Your passion once more. Thank You for Your forgiveness. Thank You for Your grace. Thank You for Your mercy. Thank You for Your strength. Release Your people to walk in the knowledge they are forgiven and they are Yours. Amen.

Challenge

Confess and repent of the sin of unbelief. Ask Holy Spirit to allow these verses to come alive. Ask him to show you why you're feeling the way you are. Deal with the root issue that's keeping you from feeling like you've been forgiven.

Declaration

I choose to forgive everyone who has wronged me. I choose to seek the forgiveness of those I have wronged. I choose to accept I have been forgiven of my confessed sin. I choose to walk in the freedom forgiveness brings.

STEP 6: LIVE UNOFFENDED AT GOD

DAY 34

Reflection

I trust my good Father to be good and do good and work all things together for the good of those he has called. I will not give him credit for the works of the one who comes to steal, kill and destroy. I see his love in everything he gives and everything he withholds. I know I trust him because he keeps me in perfect peace.

Reflection Question:

Have I been feeling perfect peace lately?

Agree to Live Without What God Withholds

Devotional

Oh, that you would rend the heavens and come down, that the mountains would tremble before you! As when fire sets twigs ablaze and causes water to boil, come down to make your name known to your enemies and cause the nations to quake before you! For when you did awesome things that we did not expect, you came down, and the mountains trembled before you. Since ancient times no one has heard, no ear has perceived, no eye has seen any God besides you, who acts on behalf of those who wait for him. You come to the help of those who gladly do right, who remember your ways. But when we continued to sin against them, you were angry. How then can we be saved? All of us have become like one who is unclean, and all our righteous acts are like filthy rags; we all shrivel up like a leaf, and like the wind our sins sweep us away. No one calls on your name or strives to lay hold of you; for you have hidden your face from us and made us waste away because of our sins. Yet, O LORD, you are our Father. We are the clay, you are the potter; we are all the work of your hand. Isaiah 64:1-8 (NIV)

Thought

I've often been asked if anyone ever needs to forgive God. That language makes me uncomfortable. Forgiveness is giving up our right for revenge. It's putting the other into the hands of God. It's His to avenge. He's the one to repay. How can we put God in His own hands? How could we ever take revenge against God?

However, forgiveness is also agreeing to live with the consequences of another's action or inaction. That could mean we may need to forgive God... but the language and sentiment isn't right.

I'm in debt to Bill Johnson for giving me biblical words to express how we need to relate to God when things happen that just don't make sense in light of His nature or character.

It comes from what John the Baptist had his disciples ask Jesus, while John sat in prison awaiting his fate.

John the Baptist declared the Lamb of God who takes away the sin of the world, knowing the Anointed One would release the prisoners. But then he sat in prison and doubt started to set in. He sent his disciples to ask his cousin if he had gotten it wrong and Jesus responded:

> "Go and tell John the things you have seen and heard: that the blind see, the lame walk, the lepers are cleansed, the deaf hear, the dead are raised, the poor have the gospel preached to them. And blessed is he who is not offended because of Me." Luke 7:22-23 (NKJV)

John was sitting where he did not expect, facing something he did not want. We could almost say he had the right to be offended at Jesus.

And Jesus said "happy is the one who is not offended because of Me."

We don't need to forgive God. We need to live un-offended with Him. Part of living un-offended at God is agreeing to live without what He withholds.

Are you in the place where your situation, through no fault of your own, is not in agreement with how the Bible says it should be?

For example, the Bible says in 1 Peter 2:24, "By His wounds we were healed." What happens when you're not?

Agreeing to live without what God withholds means we don't create theology from our experience. We can't say, "It's not God's will for me to be healed." Because we know His will is done perfectly in heaven, and we know in heaven there is no sickness, so we know it's not His will for anyone to be sick. We cannot create theology from our experience.

Agreeing to live without what God withholds means we don't make excuses for God not to be true to His word. 'Oh, in heaven I'll be healed." So does that mean in heaven you'll finally be forgiven? David said in Psalm 103, "[the Lord] forgives all your sins and heals all your diseases." Why can we believe for one and not the other in this life? Don't make excuses for God.

Agreeing to live without what God withholds does not mean we can't change God's mind. "God will heal me in His time." I know this is controversial. But look at Abraham, and Moses, and Ezekiel and Mary and how they changed God's mind. The timing of God is real, but just as real is the fact that friends of God can change His mind. The timing of God is a convenient excuse we have made a theology out of.

Agreeing to live without what God withholds means letting the potter be the potter and recognizing you are the clay. His ways are not our ways. His thoughts are not our thoughts. He thinks generationally and eternally. We are short-sighted and linear. It's best for us to simply be still and know that He is God (Psalm 46:10).

So be still, and know that He is God.

Prayer

Lord, that You would rend the heavens and come down to make Your name known and set all things right. I know You are Good and I know You are Great. And I trust You, God, to turn all things for the good of those who love You and have been called according to Your purpose. I choose to live without what You choose to withhold, knowing You are good and You are great. Amen.

Challenge

Instead of waiting for your situation to change, wait expectantly on God. Choose to still yourself by focusing on His love and goodness.

Declaration

I choose to live un-offended at God. I agree with the Bible that God is Good and God is Great. Even though I don't understand my circumstance, I give up my right to understand so that I can have the peace that passes understanding.

DAY 35

Reflection

I trust the Trustable One. I trust Him with all of my heart and have peace and joy and hope at all times and in every situation. I give up my right to understand, so I can have the peace that passes understanding. He keeps me in perfect peace because I trust in him.

Reflection Question:

Have I had peace and joy and hope lately?

Look to What God Is Doing, Not to What Is Left Undone

Devotional

"But forget all that — it is nothing compared to what I am going to do. For I am about to do something new. See, I have already begun! Do you not see it? I will make a pathway through the wilderness. I will create rivers in the dry wasteland." Isaiah 43:18-19 (NLT)

Thought

As we choose to live un-offended at God, we need to make a choice as to what we will focus on. Will our focus be on what He is doing, or will it be on what hasn't been done?

This isn't simply a case of being an optimist, a pessimist or a realist. It's a spiritual choice we make to fix our thoughts on what is true, and honourable, and right, and pure, and lovely and admirable. And to think about things that are excellent and worthy of praise (see Philippians 4:8).

We can't do that when all we see is what God hasn't done.

A tool to help us focus on the positive is testimony.

Testimony is telling the truth about God to others. It is talking about His goodness and sharing about His greatness. It is reminding ourselves of the good things He's given us and done for us.

Look how powerful testimony is. In Revelation 12:11, it talks about the saints overcoming satan:

> They overcame him by the blood of the Lamb
> and by the word of their testimony; they did not
> love their lives so much as to shrink from death.
> Revelation 12:11 (NIV)

Testimony is supernatural. Further on in Revelations chapter 19 verse 10 it says:

> ..the testimony of Jesus is the spirit of prophecy.
> Revelation 19:10 (NIV)

Remind yourself about the good things of God. Tell others about the good things of God. Fix your thoughts on what is true, and honourable, and right, and pure, and lovely and admirable. And to think about things that are excellent and worthy of praise.

Focus on what God is doing and what He has done. Don't be fixated on what He hasn't done.

Did you know someone else's testimony could open the door for us to be offended at God? It easily can if our hearts aren't right.

Bill Johnson gives an example of a group of Christians who were taken away, lined up and shot. The firing squad left and the ones on the ground got up and found holes in the shirts where the bullets entered and exited, but they had no wounds.

Incredible, right? Praise God. Amen. Send around the offering plate.

How about if your loved one was in another group of Christians who were shot, and they didn't avoid being killed? How easy would it be to ask God – why them and not my loved one? How easy would it be for a testimony to be twisted by the enemy into a weapon that opens a fresh wound?

The condition of our heart is so critical. The focus of our eyes is so essential.

Focus on what God has done and what He is doing. Take what He hasn't done to Him in prayer. He's there to comfort, but I've learned He really doesn't seem to respond well to whining.

Since my heart attack in 2019, I've come to three decisions that have changed my life and attitude.

1. **I will not give God credit for the works of the one who comes to kill steal and destroy.** John 10:10

2. **I will treat all hardship as discipline** Hebrews 12:7-11 **knowing He will work all things together for good**. Romans 8:28

3. **I will worry about nothing, pray about everything and thank Him in all things** Philippians 4:6-7 **because HE cares for me.** 1 Peter 5:7

What do those thoughts from scripture do to your perspective on your current situation?

Prayer

Lord forgive me for focusing on things You haven't done for me, instead of remembering every good and perfect gift that has come from You. Holy Spirit, help me to testify the God things of God. I agree with the word that says, "I am still confident of this,

I will see the goodness of the Lord in the land of the living. I'll be strong and take heart and wait for the Lord." Amen.

Challenge

Will you decide to not give God credit for the works of the one who comes to kill steal and destroy? Will you treat all hardship as discipline knowing He will work all things together for good? Will worry about nothing, pray about everything and thank Him in all things because HE cares for you?

Declaration

I choose to live un-offended at God. I agree with the Bible that God is Good and God is Great. Even though I don't understand my circumstance, I give up my right to understand so that I can have the peace that passes understanding.

DAY 36

Reflection

I trust in the Lord with all my heart and do not depend on my own understanding. I seek his will in all I do, and he shows me which path to take. I'm not impressed with my own wisdom. I fear the Lord and turn away from evil. I have healing for my body and strength for my bones.

Reflection Question:

Have I been seeking his will lately?

GIVE UP YOUR RIGHT TO UNDERSTAND

DEVOTIONAL

Always be full of joy in the Lord. I say it again—rejoice! Let everyone see that you are considerate in all you do. Remember, the Lord is coming soon. Don't worry about anything; instead, pray about everything. Tell God what you need, and thank him for all he has done. Then you will experience God's peace, which exceeds anything we can understand. His peace will guard your hearts and minds as you live in Christ Jesus. Philippians 4:4-7 (NLT)

Thought

When you are going through a situation that doesn't line up with the will of God expressed in Scripture, it's natural for anyone to want to make sense of it. We need to find purpose in the problem. We want to know a reason why. It's in our nature – our fallen nature – to want to make reasonable sense out of life. If we make sense of everything, where's our life of faith?

God has promised us a peace that passes understanding, but how can we expect that if we worry about trying to understand everything about what we're going through?

God's peace passes understanding. Why would we want to settle for understanding?

Asking "Why?" usually gets our focus onto what God hasn't done. We point the finger at God and others. It's counter-intuitive for living un-offended at God.

So how do we get the peace that passes understanding? I've learned to live victoriously with these principles.

STAND

S - Stop giving God credit for the works of the one who comes to steal, kill and destroy. - John 10:10

T - Treat all hardship as discipline, knowing he will work all things together for good. - Hebrews 12:7-11

A - Agree to cast all your cares upon him, because he cares for you. - 1 Peter 5:7

N - Never be lacking in zeal, but keep your spiritual fervour serving the Lord. Be joyful in hope, patient in affliction and faithful in prayer. - Romans 12:11-13

D - Don't worry about anything, but pray about everything and thank him in all things, knowing that's his will for you. - Philippians 4:6-7

Take all your concerns and leave them with God. Pray the Psalms if you need a good lament, but be sure to turn it back to the good things about God.

Wow, that sure seems like a good lesson to fast from negativity.

It does appear strange to give up the right to understand, but the secret is we can only make sense of some situations when we have the peace that passes understanding.

We don't get that peace by trying to understand.

True, at times we will make sense of some very negative events on this side of heaven. It is the glory of God to conceal a matter, and to search out a matter is the glory of kings (Proverbs 25:2).

But it's also true when we choose to live un-offended at God, sometimes understanding it all just won't matter once we have the peace that passes it.

Prayer

Lord, I need the peace that passes understanding. I call on my Lord who spoke "Peace" to the storm, and it obeyed. In my life there is a storm and I need You to change me or change my situation, or change both. Lord, I will rejoice in You always, my gentleness will be evident to all, and I will present all my requests to You with thanksgiving. You are good and You are great. Thank You, Lord. Amen.

Challenge

Rejoice, be gentle, and take everything to God with thanksgiving. Live life with the peace of God that transcends all understanding.

Declaration

I choose to live un-offended at God. I agree with the Bible that God is Good and God is Great. Even though I don't understand my circumstance, I give up my right to understand so that I can have the peace that passes understanding.

DAY 37

Reflection

I trust God with my broken dreams. I trust in his divine retribution for what the enemy has stolen. I trust he's changing me with the loss. I know he comforts me so I can comfort others with the same comfort I've been given. I trust his word that directs my steps will once again light my path. I trust him to be true to his word.

Reflection Question:

Have I been trusting or complaining lately?

Do Not Allow the Seed to Go to Waste

Devotional

I tell you the truth, unless a kernel of wheat is planted in the soil and dies, it remains alone. But its death will produce many new kernels—a plentiful harvest of new lives. Those who love their life in this world will lose it. Those who care nothing for their life in this world will keep it for eternity. John 12:24-25 (NLT)

Thought

The seed needs to die before it has any potential. Many times we stand before God with a broken dream, unfulfilled vision or loss of a promise and it feels just like the plant we tended so carefully has just gone dry and withered.

It has.

But don't let the seed go to waste.

If you bury it and water it you'll get fruit. If you sit with it and stare at it and complain about it, you'll never get the divine justice that's due because of that loss. All you do is keep the wound open and ready for infection.

Divine justice repays a loss seven times (Genesis 4:15). That's what you're entitled to as a child of the king.

It doesn't do any good to hold a seed in your hand. Plant it, water it and look for divine justice.

What if I don't care about divine justice? What if I just hurt and don't want to choose to live un-offended at God? Does it really matter?

Look at what happened to Jesus at Nazareth in Mark 6:2-5

> The next Sabbath he began teaching in the synagogue, and many who heard him were amazed. They asked, "Where did he get all this wisdom and the power to perform such miracles?" Then they scoffed, "He's just a carpenter, the son of Mary and the brother of James, Joseph, Judas, and Simon. And his sisters live right here among us." They were deeply offended and refused to believe in him. Then Jesus told them, "A prophet is honored everywhere except in his own hometown and

> among his relatives and his own family." And because of their unbelief, he couldn't do any miracles among them except to place his hands on a few sick people and heal them.

Offense at God brings unbelief. Looks what happens:

> Yes, they knew God, but they wouldn't worship him as God or even give him thanks. And they began to think up foolish ideas of what God was like. As a result, their minds became dark and confused. Claiming to be wise, they instead became utter fools. Romans 1:21-22 NLT

You may go through a season of pain, but don't let that season define your life. Don't let it rob you of your future. Plant the seed, turn the pain over to God, and trust Him to do what's right.

Water the seed – remind yourself of the truth of God's word. Insist on divine justice to repay you seven times for your loss. Know who you are in Christ and live out of the love God has for you.

Prayer

Lord, release divine justice for every area the enemy has stolen, killed and destroyed. I put my trust in You to repay and to avenge. Lord, I want this seed to spring up and produce a harvest. I want victory in the areas I've seen defeat. I want You to be recognized as true to Your word. I know that is what You are. I know You give good gifts to Your children. I rest in Your peace knowing You'll make all things right. Amen.

Challenge

Have you given way to unbelief in your life by choosing to take offence at God? Ask God to reveal any area where you have and agree with Him that what He reveals is sin. Ask for forgiveness and know you have been forgiven. Press in for divine retribution to be fully repaid.

Declaration

I choose to live un-offended at God. I agree with the Bible that God is Good and God is Great. Even though I don't understand my circumstance, I give up my right to understand so that I can have the peace that passes understanding.

STEP 7: STRENGTHEN YOURSELF IN THE LORD

DAY 38

Reflection

I strengthen myself with the Word. I have hidden his Word in my heart, so I might sin against him. His Word is life. His Word is hope. He cleanses me with his Word. It is living and active and sharper than the sharpest two-edged sword and cuts between soul and spirit, between joint and marrow. It exposes my innermost thoughts and desires. I let his Word read me.

Reflection Question:

Have I been letting his Word read me lately?

WIELD THE SWORD TO STAY STRONG

DEVOTIONAL

I lift up my hands to your commands, which I love, and I meditate on your decrees. Remember your word to your servant, for you have given me hope. My comfort in my suffering is this: Your promise preserves my life. Psalm 119:48-50 (NIV)

Thought

Jesus' words in John 16:33 were not meant to discourage us or say God is ever against those who obey Him. When He told us we'd have trouble in this world, it was a heads-up to living in a fallen world.

Since we've all experienced trouble, and since we all know there are more seasons of trouble ahead of us, the question becomes "How can we go through trouble and abstain from negativity?"

The answer is to strengthen yourself in the Lord.

This is what David did when his men returned to Ziklag to find their wives and children captured and houses destroyed and the ones who would become David's "mighty men" spoke openly about stoning him. (1 Samuel 30:6).

Over the next several days we'll look at various tools you can use to strengthen yourself in the Lord. Today we take a quick look at something most followers of Christ know they must use and very few know how to use effectively or appropriately – the living word of God.

There are three tools to remind you of, that relate to wielding the sword of the Spirit.

1. Let the Bible Read You

There are two big problems when it comes to our use of the Bible. First, we don't use it. It sits on the shelf and gathers dust. We are either intimidated to pick it up or bored with it because we think we've heard all the stories. In either case, it's an attitude of the heart we need to repent of. The Bible is our bread. It is the word that gives us life. We can't afford to not consume it regularly. Once you've repented, and in order to help you change your ways, make Bible reading a regular part of your day.

But simply reading the Bible is not enough. We can gain knowledge of the Bible, but the Bible tells us "knowledge puffs up" (1 Corinthians 8:1). So how do you read the Bible, so it has its intended effect on your life?

You let the Bible read you.

This is how you let the Bible read you.

a. Approach with reverence

b. Approach without intention

c. Approach with expectation

Maybe I should explain… please forgive a longer than usual daily encouragement… we're running out of days to talk about these topics.

a. Approach with reverence –

I fell in love with history by reading the Bible as a child. I fell more in love with the Bible, the more I studied history. This is an ancient text we amazingly have at our disposal. And it's more than that – Jesus is called the word made flesh. There was nothing in his appearance that we should be drawn to him (Isaiah 53:2-5) and though He was very God, everyone knew Him as a man. The Bible reflects Christ in this way. Although 40 different human writers wrote it over 3000 years, it is the very Word of God. So don't allow your familiarity with the Bible to breed contempt for it. It is a living and active sword.

b. Approach without intention –

If you read the Bible to prove a point, you're missing the point. If you read the Bible to say you've read it, that's the only benefit you'll receive. If you read the Bible to find your next sermon, you'll miss the treasure God has hidden for you. When you read the Bible, it is a wonderful conversation between you and the Holy Spirit.

c. Approach with expectation –

Your only intention when you read the Bible should be to hear from God. Expect Him to speak to you from His word and He will. Ask yourself questions about the passage you're reading: What did it mean for the first ones who read it? What does it mean for me? How can I apply it in my life? God will interact at your level of expectation.

When you let the Bible read you, you realize you don't consume it the Bible consumes you.

2. Meditate on the Word

Christian meditation is dramatically different from eastern meditation. The goal of eastern meditation is to empty oneself. The purpose of Christian meditation is to fill you up.

If you don't know what that means, but you do know how to worry, then you already know how to meditate on Scripture. When we worry, we think over and over and over about fears. When we meditate, we think over and over and over about faith.

Think about what the Scripture meant at the moment. Think about what it meant in the immediate context. Think about what it meant in the context of history. Think about what it meant in the context of church history. Think about what it meant for you in the past. Think about what it could mean for you in the future. Think about a picture you saw or can imagine that depicts its truth. Think about what it means for others. Think about how you could sing it. Think about how you could pray it. Commit the passage to memory. Meditation is like a cow chewing its cud. I hope you can see why.

3. Praying the Bible

In the course of this negativity fast, we've gone over how to pray the Psalms. It's a great prayer book for us to pour out our laments to God and remember to praise Him in the middle of all kinds of trouble. To strengthen yourself in the Lord, I definitely recommend the Psalms.

But the Bible gives us vocabulary for every situation we face. Don't limit yourself to the Psalms. When you pray the Bible, you pray with authority because you know you're praying the will of God. When you pray according to His will, you know He hears you, and you know you'll have what you've asked of Him.

My only warning here is to remind you to pray not only the words of the Bible, but the context of those words. And you'll only know the context as you spend the time reading the word.

When you need to strengthen yourself in the Lord, or if you need to keep your strength in the Lord, read, meditate and pray the Bible.

Prayer

Lord, You've given me Your word, so I can be thoroughly equipped for every good work. Thank You it is able to teach, rebuke, correct and train me. Holy Spirit empowers me to ensure that happens. I know that the Word of God renews my mind so that I'm able to test and approve what the good, pleasing and perfect will of God is. Forgive my lack of discipline. Help me to be consumed by Your word. Amen.

Challenge

It's not bad to have good habits but don't let habits create familiarity and familiarity breed contempt for the word of God. Read the Bible today and expect it to become alive to you.

Declaration

I choose not to be discouraged. I choose to look to God instead of my circumstance. I choose to strengthen myself in the Lord.

DAY 39

Reflection

I remember to remember to the good things God has done. I remember His encouragement, His strengthening and His miracles. I remember I have been through the waters and he has been with me. I have passed through the rivers and I have not been drowned. I have walked through the fire, and not be burned, the flames did not set me ablaze. He has been so good to me.

Reflection Question:

What's something God entrusted to me that I haven't thought about lately?

REMEMBERING TO REMEMBER

DEVOTIONAL

"Whenever the rainbow appears in the clouds, I will see it and remember the everlasting covenant between God and all living creatures of every kind on the earth." Genesis 9:16 (NIV)

Thought

In ancient times, a sign of a covenant was the one making the promise would turn the bow around so an arrow would face him, if it was "loaded." He'd pull the string and declare the oath. This was a way to say, "If I break this covenant, my life is forfeit."

God did exactly the same thing when He gave Noah and all creation the rainbow in the sky. It's as if He's holding the bow against himself every time the rainbow appears.

I love rainbows. They remind me to remember that God is really, really good.

When in this world we have trouble, or even when we choose busy-ness to rule in our lives, remembering to remember is the first thing we forget.

Let's never forget the power of testimony.

Marketing mavens know the value of a "social proof." You need to have testimonials of your products or services on your website. But for the follower of Christ, testimony is even more powerful. BTW... feel to leave what you think about the Negativity Fast at **http://revtrev.link/mystory**. I really appreciate hearing what you have to say.

Testimony literally means the "story, or report, of one."

Testimony is powerful because it is immediate, direct and personal. It isn't a story about something or a report about what somebody else said or did. It's not a theory or hypothesis or hope. It is a personal description of your own direct experience.

So how often do you remember the good things God has done for you?

This is one area I need to improve on. God can bring to my memory incredible things He's done for me... and He often does when I wait on Him and listen to what He says. But most of the things I journal are in the dark days of my life. I write when I finally realize I can't do anything but cry out to God. And too often I forget to write down His answer. I've learned to write down his answer for my own encouragement.

Testimony is a powerful tool for us to use to remember. So keep a spiritual journal. What is God telling you today? What is He revealing to you? What verses came alive to you? If you keep track of your prayer requests, keep track of their answers as well. If you write out your laments like the Psalms, remember to praise Him for answers that have come. I often put updates in my personal journals, but to do so, I need to remember to read the journal regularly. That may help you as well. Take time to remember by reading your journal.

Now testimony is great for us as individuals, but its true power comes in community. If you have an accountability partner, hold each other accountable to talk about the good things God is doing. Be accountable for positivity. When there's opportunity to share in your church or on the street – make the most of it, remembering to do it with gentleness and respect. That's why you have a story to remember.

Your story influences others to trust God and praise God and turn to God in their own circumstance. It doesn't matter if you've been a follower of Christ for decades or have just begun the journey today, your story is important.

The most fun I have in life is to talk to new believers who bring newness to truths that I have taken for granted. Visiting with seniors who share their stories of God's goodness is also great... come to think of it – I like being around people who talk about the good things of God.

I need to be one of those people so people around me will be more like those kinds of people as well.

Will you be one?

Sharing with others your personal interactions with God enables you to strengthen yourself in the Lord.

Prayer

Lord, help me to remember the good things You've done. Spirit, empower me to tell others about how good You are. I know it helps me to strengthen myself in You and I know it releases something in the heavens, because even angels long to look into the mysteries of God. Amen.

Challenge

Start a journal today, or write in your journal today. Make it a journal to remember the goodness of God. Record what you can remember from your past, or write down what God is revealing to you today. Write in it regularly and read it often.

Declaration

I choose not to be discouraged. I choose to look to God instead of my circumstance. I choose to strengthen myself in the Lord.

DAY 40

Reflection

I choose to praise him before the battle starts. I praise him before my answer comes. I praise him in the middle of the storm. I praise him because he is worthy of praise. I praise him because it changes me. I am never impressed with the size of my problem when I'm impressed with the glory of my God.

Reflection Question:

Have I chosen to praise him lately?

CHOOSING PRAISE

DEVOTIONAL

After consulting the people, Jehoshaphat appointed men to sing to the LORD and to praise him for the splendor of his holiness as they went out at the head of the army, saying: "Give thanks to the LORD, for his love endures forever." 2 Chronicles 20:18 (NIV)

Thought

When we face discouragement, many times the discouragement comes in the form of worry. So here are some quick steps to help you worry less and strengthen yourself in the Lord:

1. **Isolate the worries that are on your mind the most.** These are often the worries that we think about as we are falling asleep or as we wake in the morning.

2.

Ask yourself specifically what you are afraid of. This will be the lie you are choosing to believe.

3. **Ask yourself what the outcome would be of this specific fear coming true.**

4. **Ask God to show you the truth about the situation.**

5. **Ask God what He would have you do.**

6. **Expect God to answer you.**

7. **Replace the lie with the truth God revealed.**

8. **Obey what God tells you to do.**

These eight-steps fit well with **2 Chronicles 20.** Judah was facing three armies coming against them.

1. It was easy for them to isolate the worries. **(v.2-4)**

2. Jehoshaphat called out to God on behalf of the people and specifically voiced what they were concerned about. **(v.10)**

3. He looked at the outcome of the specific fear coming true. **(v.11)**

4. He reminded everyone about the truth of God. **(v.6)**

5. He ended his prayer with a cry we can all use: "We

don't know what to do, but our eyes are upon you." **(v.12)**

6. A prophetic word came out as God's answer to the impending doom **(v.15-17)**. This answer is also often ours – "You will not have to fight this battle. Take up your positions; stand firm and see the deliverance the LORD will give you." **(v.17)**

7. They worshipped God in response to His revelation, and then Jehoshaphat replaced the lies of the enemy with the truth of God by declaring, "Listen to me, Judah and people of Jerusalem! Have faith in the LORD your God and you will be upheld; have faith in his prophets and you will be successful." **(v.20)**

8. Then they sent singers ahead of the army to praise God for who He is as they went out to obey what He told them to do. **(v.21)**

The result for Judah was that there was no need to worry. God was in control. He set ambushes for the enemy, and they destroyed themselves.

When we can get to the place of praising God for who He is before the things we worry about come to reality, they won't materialize.

Now I can hear the skeptic smirk, "most things people worry about never come about."

True. So stop worrying completely by praising God continually.

That's the 1-step program I intended to tell you about until God led me to 2 Chronicles 20.

Praise is our natural response to the goodness of God. When we see God as good, how can we worry about anything bad?

> Let all I am praise the Lord; may I never forget the good things he does for me. Psalm 103:2

We can't. Strengthen yourself in the Lord by choosing praise.

Prayer

Lord, I praise You now, even though I may not feel like it. Telling You the truth about Yourself reminds me how truly good You are. As I focus more on Your goodness my praise becomes more natural. You are good and Your love endures forever. You are good and Your mercies are renewed every morning. You are good and altogether trustworthy. You are good. You are good. You are good. You are good. You are good. You are good. You are good. Thanks for being so good. Amen

Challenge

Read 2 Chronicles 20 and look for more of the treasures in this passage. Pray Psalm 86 and take extra time to praise God for who He is.

Declaration

I choose not to be discouraged. I choose to look to God instead of my circumstance. I choose to strengthen myself in the Lord.

DAY 41

Reflection

I ask for wisdom and I get wisdom. Wisdom I get is from above. It is first of all pure. It is also peace loving, gentle at all times, and willing to yield to others. It is full of mercy and the fruit of good deeds. It shows no favouritism and is always sincere. I seek his will in all I do and seek first his kingdom and righteousness.

Reflection Question:

Have I asked God for wisdom lately?

STANDING IN THE COUNCIL OF GOD

DEVOTIONAL

But if they had stood in my council, they would have proclaimed my words to my people and would have turned them from their evil ways and from their evil deeds. Jeremiah 23:22 (NIV)

Thought

There is one sermon I often hear preached that I just can't agree with. It is divisive to evangelistic outreach, ignores the context of Scripture, and it's ignorant of the plans and purposes of God.

Yet the main point it makes is true... it's just based on the wrong text.

Now, don't lambaste your pastor if he ever preaches, "Don't have an Ishmael" because in this fast from negativity you should be in the habit of only speaking words that build up. It's not my intention to cause divisions with this illustration. Most preachers just don't read the text, God will hold them to account – you don't have to.

The basic premise of the sermon is, "don't get ahead of God." Great, I agree.

That's not what Abraham did though:

In Genesis 13, God told Abram his offspring would be like the dust of the earth – no one could count them. In Chapter 15, God confirmed the offspring would come from Abram's own body. In Chapter 16, Abram's wife Sarai offered her maidservant to fulfill a culturally legitimate function that God honoured in the creation of the twelve patriarchs, two generations later. In Chapter 17, God finally told the newly named Abraham, Sarah would have a son AND that God would bless Ishmael (v.20).

That's really not the topic of today's thought, simply something we need to change in the church if we're ever going to see Islam go the way of Communism before Christ returns. God loves the children of Ishmael, and is waiting for their full number to come in.

"Don't get ahead of God" is a true message. Jesus only said what He heard the Father say and only did what He heard the Father do (John 5:19-20). Do you think Christ's times of getting away to pray had anything to do with it?

"Don't get ahead of God" isn't a license to stay stagnant. It's a challenge to listen and obey. When you stand in the council of God, He tells you the words to say, He gives you the love to show, He provides the strategies you need. (Jeremiah 23:22)

When we listen with expectancy, we hear the voice of God. When we hear God, we are encouraged. When we hear God, we are blessed. When we hear God, we know who we are. Waiting to hear the voice of God is another way to strengthen ourselves in the Lord.

So make the time to expectantly listen... then go until God says, "no."

Prayer

Father, I come in the name of Jesus Christ with thanksgiving and praise. As I wait upon You now, I do my best to listen to Your voice. I stand before the almighty God and seek Your counsel. Please reveal any information that I need for today. Reveal any strategies that I need to employ right now. I need to be knowing and doing what You want. Amen.

Challenge

Spend time in the presence of God. Expect Him to speak. Wait for Him to speak. Do what He says... it will always be in line with His will expressed in Scripture.

Declaration

I choose not to be discouraged. I choose to look to God instead of my circumstance. I choose to strengthen myself in the Lord.

DAY 42

Reflection

I build myself up in the most holy faith, praying in the Holy Spirit. I don't know what I say, but Holy Spirit prays through me. As I pray, though my mind is unfruitful, I build myself up. I think about what is good and right and honourable and worthy of praise. I pray in faith knowing the Spirit helps me in my weakness.

Reflection Question:

Have I prayed in the Spirit lately?

PRAY IN THE SPIRIT

DEVOTIONAL

But you, dear friends, build yourselves up in your most holy faith and pray in the Holy Spirit. Jude 1:20 (NIV)

Thought

Did you ever notice Paul wished everyone would speak in tongues? Read 1 Corinthians 14:5 a little slower, and stop at the first comma. If you jump up to the verse 4, you'll see why... because the ones who speak in tongues build themselves up.

The context of 1 Corinthians 11 – 14 is that Paul is addressing problems that happen when the church is gathered. When you speak in tongues, it's for God and yourself. It's not for other people (14:2) so it doesn't need to be done in a public gathering.

However, much of our public gathering today is focused on a personal intimate time with God. Since speaking in tongues builds yourself up, if it's appropriate in your church context, why not pray to God in an unknown language much like you would in a language that you've learned?

That's a sidebar... let's get back to how to strengthen yourself in the Lord.

Paul taught the church in Rome:

> In the same way, the Spirit helps us in our weakness. We do not know what we ought to pray for, but the Spirit himself intercedes for us with groans that words cannot express. And he who searches our hearts knows the mind of the Spirit, because the Spirit intercedes for the saints in accordance with God's will. Romans 8:26-27 (NIV)

Allowing the Spirit to pray through us allows us to pray confidently knowing we intercede for others according to the will of God. It allows us to pray beyond words, because we don't know what to pray, but the Spirit Himself intercedes for us.

But is it for everyone?

In 1 Corinthians 12:31, 14:1 and 14:39, we are told to "eagerly desire greater" spiritual gifts. In the context of the passage, the greater gifts are the gifts that fit the moment. For example, prophecy is more desirable for a group setting, so seek to prophesy when you're together. Since speaking in tongues builds up the individual, we can assume when we're alone the greater gift is the gift of tongues.

Why would Paul want everyone to speak in tongues if it was not available to everyone? Why would he say to not forbid the speaking in tongues (1 Corinthians 14:39) if we all couldn't do it? Why are we told to build ourselves up as we pray in the Holy Spirit (Jude 1:20) if it's only available for some?

When you eagerly desire the gifts of the Spirit, it only takes a moment before you begin to operate in those gifts. The key is expectancy.

Luke 11:9-13 says:

> So I say to you: Ask and it will be given to you; seek and you will find; knock and the door will be opened to you. For everyone who asks receives; he who seeks finds; and to him who knocks, the door will be opened. "Which of you fathers, if your son asks for a fish, will give him a snake instead? Or if he asks for an egg, will give him a scorpion? If you then, though you are evil, know how to give

> good gifts to your children, how much more will your Father in heaven give the Holy Spirit to those who ask him!" (NIV)

God is good and He gives good gifts to His children. Eagerly desire the gifts of the Spirit and the Spirit will give them.

So to strengthen yourself in the Lord pray in tongues if you've got them, seek them if you don't.

Prayer

Lord, You are the giver of good gifts. I'm asking You for your best. I know in this life I need to build myself up in You and since the gift of tongues is the gift You've provided Your body to do just that, I ask You for this gift and I will eagerly pursue all gifts You give for the good of Your body and bride. Amen.

Challenge

Most people's problem with speaking in tongues is psychological, not spiritual. We expect the Holy Spirit to possess us and move our lips. It rarely happens that way. God is a gentleman and won't impose His will on us. You're going to need to open your mouth. You're going to need to form words you don't understand with your lips. Since without faith it's impossible to please God, when you do this by faith, you know you're pleasing Him.

If you can already speak in tongues, pray using them for 20 minutes a day and see how strengthened you become over the next week.

Declaration

I choose not to be discouraged. I choose to look to God instead of my circumstance. I choose to strengthen myself in the Lord.

STEP 8: CHANGE YOUR EVERYDAY WORLD

DAY 43

REFLECTION

My light shines bright. I change the atmosphere around me. My smile brightens every room. My demeanour lifts the clouds off of others. It's not me, but Holy Spirit in me that does the work and spreads the grace. My presence brings his presence and in his presence is fullness of joy.

Reflection Question:

How have people commented on what I bring into the room lately?

CHANGE THE WEATHER

But the LORD said to Moses and Aaron, "Because you did not trust in me enough to honour me as holy in the sight of the Israelites, you will not bring this community into the land I give them." Numbers 20:12 (NIV)

Thought

God almost always punished the children of Israel when they grumbled against Him as they spent the 40 years wondering in the desert. There was one time He didn't. Instead, He punished Moses – the one who interceded for the people time and time and time again.

It was the time Moses' reaction to the sin of the people was in direct disobedience to what God told him to do. Look at Numbers chapter 20. The people once again complained to Moses. He went before God and was told to lift up his rod over the rock. Instead, he struck it twice and was told he wouldn't bring the people into the land of promise.

Seems a bit harsh, doesn't it?

Maybe we should see how seriously God takes our response to negative situations. Moses' reaction to the complaints of the people made him sin against God.

Do we ever allow our negative circumstances to let us choose to sin against God?

One of the lessons God teaches me every time I do a negativity fast is I need to be careful how I react to actions, attitudes and spirits that set themselves up against the knowledge of Christ. When people who should know better seem to act under the spirit of stupor I want to confront them and challenge them and get them to see it right... I need to digress; I'm fasting from negativity and as you can see, I may have a way to go to make it a lifestyle.

I know how God wants me to react. I'll share more of that in about two days. But for now it's enough for you to know that how we react to those around us is important to God.

Moses couldn't enter the promise land because of how he reacted to the grumbling of the people of Israel.

So how are we to act positively in extremely negative situations?

The key is to practice the presence of God.

Brother Lawrence was a 16th century Carmelite monk and was the first to popularize this discipline. He saw God in everything. All his work was "as unto the Lord." He wrote in what would become "The Practice of the Presence of God":

> "As often as I could, I placed myself as a worshiper before Him, fixing my mind upon His holy presence, recalling it when I found it wandering from Him. This proved to be an exercise frequently painful, yet I persisted through all difficulties."

Practicing the presence of God is focusing on His holy presence wherever we are, whatever we do. When you live within a negative environment, you need to live with the understanding given to us by JB Philips' translation of Romans 12:1-3:

> "Don't let the world around you squeeze you into its own mold, but let God remold your minds from within, so that you may prove in practice that the plan of God for you is good, meets all his demands, and moves toward the goal of true maturity" Romans 12:1-3 (Phillips)

Don't use your negative environment as an excuse to remain negative. As a child of the one who created the weather, you bring your own weather wherever you go. As you allow God to renew your mind from within, you will begin to change the world around you.

You are the salt of the world and light of the earth. You preserve and illuminate the area where you are. The gates of hell cannot prevail against you so live the promise of Isaiah 26:3:

> You will keep in perfect peace all who trust in you,
> all whose thoughts are fixed on you! (NLT)

Prayer

Lord, I know it matters to You how I respond to other people's negativity. Forgive me for responding negatively to their negativity. Help me, Holy Spirit, to recognize the holiness of God wherever I go. Enable me, loving God, to bring Your love, joy, peace, patience, kindness, goodness, faithfulness and self-control wherever I go. Amen.

Challenge

Take up the 16th century challenge of Brother Lawrence and as often as you can today, place yourself before God as a worshipper and fix your thoughts on His goodness and holiness. Bring Him into your thoughts and conversation today.

Declaration

I choose to change my negative environment by seeking God and pursuing His peace.

DAY 44

REFLECTION

I pursue the presence of God. I learn His unforced rhythms of grace. It's His presence that distinguishes me from all the people of the earth. I know He is in me and around and upon me and before me and behind me. I feel Him all around me and I wait for Him to speak to my spirit.

Reflection Question:

Have I waited in His presence lately?

PURSUING THE PALPABLE PRESENCE OF GOD

DEVOTIONAL

You reveal the path of life to me; in Your presence is abundant joy; in Your right hand are eternal pleasures. Psalm 16:11 (HCSB)

Thought

If you've been reading the articles I've written on how to fast from negativity, you'll know that I'm a big fan of spending time in the palpable presence of God.

Call it soaking, waiting, marinating, shut up and listen time, or whatever... I'm convinced it is a key for keeping in step with the Spirit and carrying only the burdens Christ has for us. It changes us, so we can change our environment.

Pursuing the palpable presence is where you quit striving, you focus on the love of God and you expect God to speak. Let the word of God guide you. Let the music encourage you. Tell God you're waiting until you know He's released you to move on, and you wait knowing He's going to speak and that you'll need to respond.

I don't know if Moses had the music, but he had the sentiment in Exodus 33:

> Then Moses said to him [the Lord], "If your Presence does not go with us, do not send us up from here. How will anyone know that you are pleased with me and with your people unless you go with us? What else will distinguish me and your people from all the other people on the face of the earth?" Exodus 33:15-16 (NIV)

It's not the power of God we seek; it's the presence of God that distinguishes us from all the other people on the face of the earth. In His presence there is fullness of joy and the joy of the Lord is our strength. It's in His presence that we can see things from His perspective. It's in His presence that burdens are lifted.

If we don't make time to experience the palpable presence of God we will not carry the yoke that is easy and the burden that is light.

Read how Eugene Peterson translates Matthew 11:28-30

> "Are you tired? Worn out? Burned out on religion? Come to me. Get away with me, and you'll recover your life. I'll show you how to take a real rest. Walk with me and work with me—watch how I do it. Learn the unforced rhythms of grace. I won't lay anything heavy or ill-fitting on you. Keep company with me, and you'll learn to live freely and lightly." (The Message)

That's the benefit of pursuing the palpable presence of God. Learn the unforced rhythms of grace. Learn to live freely and lightly. It is so great to make use of our rights as children of the King. Go spend some time on your Daddy's lap.

Prayer

Lord, give me an expectant heart. I need to believe what Your word says is true – that I'll seek You and find You when I seek You with all of my heart. I know that as I wait expectantly on You, I'll renew my strength and rise up with wings as eagles. I'll run and not grow weary, I'll walk and not faint. Lord, teach me to wait expectantly. Amen.

Challenge

Make time today to cease striving. Be still and know that He is God. Play some worshipful music. Meditate on a passage of scripture. Focus on the love of God. Expect Him to speak.

Declaration

I choose to change my negative environment by seeking God and pursuing His peace.

DAY 45

Reflection

I have peace at all times and in every situation. Peace is proof I trust my Father. I cast my cares on Him because I know He cares for me. He keeps me in perfect peace because I trust in him. The God of all hope fills me with peace and joy, so I can overflow with hope by the power of Holy Spirit.

Reflection Question:

Where has my peace been lately?

PEACE IS THE PROOF OF YOUR AUTHORITY

DEVOTIONAL

Don't be intimidated in any way by your enemies. This will be a sign to them that they are going to be destroyed, but that you are going to be saved, even by God himself. Philippians 1:28 (NLT)

Thought

When God places us as His salt and light in an environment that is extremely negative, our peace can change the weather around us. Peace isn't being self-assured; it's being assured that God is good.

Francis Frangipane wrote in an email concerning spiritual warfare:

> We will never know Christ's victory in its fullness until we stop reacting humanly to our circumstances. When you truly have authority over something, you can look at that thing without worry, fear or intimidation. Your peace is the proof of your victory.

The disciples were scared at the storm on the lake, while Jesus slept in peace (Matthew 8:23-27). When they woke Him up He didn't fight against the storm or fear it. He used His authority in perfect peace.

When did Jesus ever argue with demons? Even satan was simply answered with truth.

Jesus was so calm as He stood before Pilate that in a matter of moments, it was no longer Jesus who was on trial, but satan, Pilate and the religious establishment in Israel.

Francis Frangipane continued:

> Satan's arsenal consists of such things as fear, worry, doubt and self-pity. Every one of these weapons robs us of peace and leaves us troubled inside. Do you want to discern where the enemy is coming against you? In the network of your relationships, wherever you do not have peace--you have war. Conversely, wherever you

> have peace--you have victory. When satan hurls his darts against you, the more peace you have during adversity, the more truly you are walking in Christ's victory.

Paul told the Philippians:

> Don't be intimidated in any way by your enemies. This will be a sign to them that they are going to be destroyed, but that you are going to be saved, even by God himself. Philippians 1:28 (NLT)

He's saying that our peace is a sign to others that God is in control, and we're on the winning side. You'll remember a couple of days ago I confessed I need to be careful how I react to actions, attitudes and spirits that set themselves up against the knowledge of Christ. I tend to get aggressive and confrontational. At least I did, until God decided to teach me more about peace. He's doing it by showing me Jesus.

Jesus was never in a hurry. He ignored ignorant arguments. He took time for people. He took time to laugh. Even the darkest moments He spent in prayer. He was overwhelmed with grief, but never crushed. He never used His circumstance as an excuse to step out of the will of God. It's tough to understand His peace.

That's the kind of peace I'm after, and it's the kind of peace I get when I live out Philippians 4:4-8.

We'll conclude with Francis Frangipane's conclusion:

> Rest precedes rule. Peace precedes power. Do not seek to rule over the devil until you are submitting to God's rule over you. The focal point of all victory comes from seeking God until you find Him, and having found Him, allowing His presence to fill your spirit with His peace. From full assurance at His right hand, as you rest in His victory, so will you rule in the midst of your enemies.

So seek peace and pursue it.

Prayer

Lord, I know You are the God of peace and have peace that passes understanding available to me as I rejoice, am gentle, am thankful and take everything to You in prayer. Spirit, help me to always fix my thoughts on what is true, and honourable, and right, and pure, and lovely and admirable. Help me to think about things that are excellent and worthy of praise so that Christ's authority in me can be seen. Amen.

Challenge

Seek peace by seeking God. Allow His presence to fill you with His peace. Don't be intimated by people and circumstance. Spend time with God to be reminded He is good, and He is great.

Declaration

I choose to change my negative environment by seeking God and pursuing His peace.

DAY 46

Reflection

I do everything in love. I speak the truth in love. I am patient. I am kind. I am not jealous or boastful or proud or rude. I do not demand my own way. I am not irritable, and I keep no record of being wronged. I am unoffendable. I do not rejoice over injustice, but I rejoice whenever the truth wins out. I never give up. I never lose faith. I am always hopeful, and endure through every circumstance.

Reflection Question:

Have I been doing everything in love lately?

DO EVERYTHING IN LOVE

DEVOTIONAL

We know what real love is because Jesus gave up his life for us. So we also ought to give up our lives for our brothers and sisters. If someone has enough money to live well and sees a brother or sister in need but shows no compassion—how can God's love be in that person? Dear children, let's not merely say that we love each other; let us show the truth by our actions. Our actions will show that we belong to the truth, so we will be confident when we stand before God. Even if we feel guilty, God is greater than our feelings, and he knows everything. Dear friends, if we don't feel guilty, we can come to God with bold confidence. And we will receive from him whatever we ask because we obey him and do the things that please him. And this is his commandment: We must believe in the name of his Son, Jesus Christ, and love one another, just as he commanded us. 1 John 3:16-23 (NLT)

Thought

It's really difficult to say more about love than John does in his first letter. The man was passionate about love. I'm convinced it was because the church in Ephesus - that he was an elder of - was told by God to return to their first love or else they would cease to exist.

I'm sure I wrote more about that somewhere, and I'm sure it's really good stuff, but I can't find it in all this information that's been produced as I've tried to help people fast from negativity. In some ways, it has been a long journey, so it's good to reflect on the final day and say with Qoheleth:

> That's the whole story. Here now is my final conclusion: Fear God and obey his commands, for this is everyone's duty. Ecclesiastes 12:13 (NLT)

What is God's command? – To love God and love others. Love is the fulfillment of the law. Love is the antidote to negativity.

"Love God, love others" sounds so simple, and it is. But if it were easy to love, why wouldn't more people do it?

The answer to that question is also simple. It means death to ourselves when we put other people's interests ahead of our own. It means death to ourselves when we change our negative thinking patterns. It means death to ourselves when we speak words of life and stop speaking words of death. It means death to ourselves when we reflect the goodness of God to the side of the world that's away from the Son.

And that's the kind of sacrifice Jesus is looking for. He said in Luke 14:26-27:

> "If anyone comes to me and does not hate his father and mother, his wife and children, his brothers and sisters—yes, even his own life—he cannot be my disciple. And anyone who does not carry his cross and follow me cannot be my disciple."

Christ is worthy of a greater love than the earliest love, a greater love than the dearest love, and a greater love than the nearest love.

Will you give it to Him today and always?

Will you show your love for Him by the way you love others?

You've been doing it for this negativity fast. When you've messed up, you've confessed and God's forgiven you. You know how to do it and you know it can be done. You can do all things through Christ who gives you strength.

This is not the end of the journey. **Stay on the path we've joined for this short time.** Why not join the Live LIGHT Friends group on Facebook for free

https://revtrev.com/friends or get all the courses and all the resources and the full community on LiveLIGHT.ca at the best price right now – **https://livelight.ca/pathway**

So before we part, I want to pray for you. I know I've prayed it over you often in my times with God. It's Paul's prayer to the Ephesians:

> I keep asking that the God of our Lord Jesus Christ, the glorious Father, may give you the Spirit of wisdom and revelation, so that you may know him better. I pray also that the eyes of your heart may be enlightened in order that you may know the hope to which he has called you, the riches of his glorious inheritance in the saints, and his incomparably great power for us who believe.
> Ephesians 1:17-19 (NIV)

You are loved by God, so love loving others… He does.

Prayer

Lord, I thank You for all You taught me and have shown me on this 40-day journey. Specifically, I want to thank You for (Fill in the Blank). You are good and You are great. I thank You. I thank You for Your love. I thank You for Your mercy. I thank You for

Your grace. I thank You that You empower me to love others in Your name. Amen.

Challenge

Celebrate God today. Take some time to go over Isaiah 58 and reflect on the fast you've just completed. Focus on the promises in that text. Know that great things are in store. Remember the things He's spoken to you or provided for you or shown you these past 40 days. Talk about them to others. Rejoice a great deal today.

Declaration

I can do all things through Christ who strengthens me!

BONUS DAY

Reflection

I remember the deeds of the Lord; yes, I remember what he's done in my life. Let all that I am praise the Lord; with my whole heart, I will praise his holy name. Let all that I am praise the Lord; may I never forget the good things he does for me. He has redeemed my life from the pit and crowned me love and compassion.

Reflection Question:

What has God done for me on this journey?

CONSIDER AND CELEBRATE

CELEBRATION!

My counsel for you is simple and straightforward: Just go ahead with what you've been given. You received Christ Jesus, the Master; now live him. You're deeply rooted in him. You're well constructed upon him. You know your way around the faith. Now do what you've been taught. School's out; quit studying the subject and start living it! And let your life spill over into thanksgiving. Colossians 2:6 (The Message)

Thought

Congratulations! You've made it! How did you do with the Checkpoints and Milestones? Did anything surprise you? Are you excited?

I know we can't cover everything in these reflections and devotionals, so I created the **Live LIGHT Above the**

Negativity Course to help you take thoughts captive, demolish strongholds and tear down imaginations that set themselves up against the knowledge of Christ.

Do you want to go deeper? Get the best price for the Live LIGHT Above the Negativity course **http://revtrev.link/bless**

I've also created the **Live LIGHT Pathway** Get ALL the Courses and ALL the resources and the Full Community Live LIGHT Pathway Course and Community today at **https://livelight.ca/pathway**

Finally, I know people may want to go through this fast again. I think it's easier as a course. You have access to it for as long as you want to keep an account on LiveLIGHT.ca. I also know once people go through it, they often want to take others through it. Get the best price at **http://revtrev.link/fast**

Do you want to do it again with friends and family or co-workers? You can do another negativity fast with others whenever you want. Here's some tips to help with that.

FAST

F - Figure out who you'll do it with

A - Agree to a season that works for everyone (it's 47 days)

S - Strategies how you'll do it together (FB group? weekly coffee? daily group chats?)

T - Together, sign up for the Reflections and Devotions - (Start on the same day- you may need to use another email address if you want the Reflections in your inbox)

Can I pray for you?

Lord, I thank you for everyone who made it this far and all the ones who will take it in the future. Help us to remember that we can have peace and joy and hope at all times and in every situation because of who you are and what you have done for us. Amen.

Until next time

Carpe Vitae!

GET THE LIVE LIGHT PATHWAY - ALL THE COURSES AND RESOURCES AND THE FULL LIVE LIGHT COMMUNITY

Would you like the course that goes with this book? How about the supporting course that goes deeper to Live LIGHT Above the Negativity with your whole heart? Blessings from the Book and Live LIGHT with Your Whole Heart is also included. More courses are being developed all the time. Check out all you get today included – Coaching, Community, Courses, and resources. https://livelight.ca/pathway

The Live LIGHT Pathway includes **ALL THE Courses and All the Resources on LiveLIGHT.ca** AND the FULL **Live LIGHT Pathway Community** - the Private Facebook Group as well as Community on LiveLIGHT.ca

Sign up today! https://livelight.ca/pathway

7 PRINCIPLES OF LIVE LIGHT

The 7 Principles of Live LIGHT can be most easily remembered with the word FREEDOM

F - Firm Foundation

R - Real Responsibility

E - Effortless Transformation

E - Emotions are Key

D - Decidedly Wholehearted

O - Open and Life-Giving Community

M - Manifest Peace

Firm Foundation

God is good and He's in a good mood. People need to be dependent on God, not dependent on us. When they can hear God for themselves, lies are ripped from the roots. Our ambition is to love always and help anyone who seeks, to have well-healed wounds. Courses and resources and community and coaching is what we offer to help. Everything we offer is designed to HELP - Honour, Empower, and be Life-giving and Pleasing to God. It's true. It's helpful. It's focused. It solves a problem. It's action-orientated.

Real Responsibility

We hold people capable and know Holy Spirit is trustable to finish the good work he's started in us. He has given us everything we need for life and godliness. He empowers us to accomplish every good work prompted by faith. In love, we can't help anyone more than they want to help themselves.

Effortless Transformation

Information is only as good as the transformation it helps facilitate. Transformation is Holy Spirit's work. It happens when we move from order, to disorder, to reorder. Transformation becomes easy when we replace the lie-based beliefs with the truth God speaks to us.

Emotions are Key

Emotions are terrible masters but excellent servants. Our emotions tell us what we really believe. We do not focus entirely on behaviour or symptoms, but rather on lie-based beliefs. When people find freedom from the lies they believe, the symptoms caused by their lie-based thinking simply goes away.

Decidedly Wholehearted

Our heart is the seat of our decision, the seat of our action and the seat of our emotions. When these aren't in agreement, there is cognitive dissonance and/or toxic behaviour. We are double-minded and unstable. We can learn and practice to do everything we do unto the Lord and with our whole heart as we replace the lie-based beliefs with the truth God speaks to us.

Open and Life-Giving Community

When people are hurt in community, they need to be healed in community. Transformation often takes place over time and transformation usually takes place best over time in a life-giving community. We make it simple for people we work with to pass on what we impart to others. We focus on simple, effective courses, resources, community and coaching that enable people to bless and train others in their everyday world.

Manifest Peace

Peace is the only emotion we can allow to rule in our heart. Because we have peace with God, we can have peace with others - as far as it depends on us - and peace with ourselves. Anything that costs us our peace is too expensive. The God of hope fills us with peace and joy as we trust in him, so we can overflow with hope by the power of Holy Spirit. When peace rules our heart, it rules our emotions, our decisions and our actions and we live whole hearted. The world needs the peace we have to share.

LIVE LIGHT MANIFESTO

FOR ALL THOSE WHO ARE CALLED TO FREEDOM AND USE FREEDOM TO SERVE OTHERS IN LOVE. GALATIANS 5:13

Download your printable copy at **https://livelight.ca/downloads**

I was created to walk with God in the garden in the cool of the day. **Genesis 3:8**

Sin came into the world and I bore the consequences. **Romans 6:23**

Jesus came and reversed the curse **Galatians 3:13** and took my place **Titus 2:14** and invited me to take his yoke that is easy and his burden that is light. **Matthew 11:28-30**

I am a child of God creation longs to be revealed. **Romans 8:19**

I am a living LIGHT. **Matthew 5:14-16**

I don't conform. I am being transformed. **Romans 12:2**

I live out of my God-created identity. **1 John 3:1**

I make it my ambition to lead a quiet life. **1 Thessalonians 4:11-12** I want His peace at all times in every situation. **2 Thessalonians 3:16**

I don't have time to be busy. **Luke 8:14**

I don't have time to worry. **Philippians 4:6-7**

I don't have time to waste. **Ephesians 5:16-17**

I can't love God and show. **Matthew 6:2;16**

I can't love God and dough. **Matthew 6:24**

I can't love God and worry. **Matthew 6:25-32**

I can't love God and hurry. **Matthew 6:34**

I know priority can never be plural. **Matthew 6:33**

My whole heart aligns my decisions and actions and emotions. **Philippians 4:8-9**

My emotions show me what I actually believe. **Luke 6:45**

He empowers me to accomplish ever good work prompted by faith. **2 Thessalonians 1:11**

I take my everyday life, my eating, sleeping, going-to-work, and walking-around life and lay it before him as an offering. **Romans 12:1**

I only do what i see the Father do. **John 5:19** I only say what I hear the Father say. **John 12:49**

I do everything as unto the Lord. **Colossians 3:23-24** Faith is my natural response to His revelation. **Hebrews 11:6**

I take thoughts captive, I tear down strongholds, I demolish arguments. **2 Corinthians 10:4-5**

I will not give God credit for the works of the one who comes to kill steal and destroy. **John 10:10** I will treat all hardship as discipline **Hebrews 12:7-11** knowing He will work all things together for good. **Romans 8:28** I will worry about nothing, pray about everything and thank Him in all things **Philippians 4:6-7** because HE cares for me. **1 Peter 5:7**

I choose to be interruptible **Luke 8:43-48** and unoffendable. **1 Corinthians 13:4-7**

I choose to wholeheartedly Live LIGHT. **Matthew 5:15-16**

I choose to Live Loved **1 John 4:19**, knowing nothing can separate me from His love. **Romans 8:38-39** Jesus said, "Make yourselves at home in my love." **John 15:9**

I choose to Live Intentional **Ephesians 5:15-17**, the way Jesus only said **John 12:49** and did what came from the Father. **John 5:19** Jesus said, "I only do what I see the Father doing." John 5:19

I choose to Live Generous **1 John 3:17**, the way God lives towards everyone. **Matthew 5:45** Jesus said, "Give away your life." **Luke 6:38**

I choose to Live Hopeful **Romans 12:12**, knowing I can trust my good Father **1 Thessalonians 5:24**. Jesus said, "Don't get lost in despair..." **John 14:1**

I choose to Live Today **Matthew 6:34**, knowing faithfulness to God is multiplication. **Matthew 25:14-30** Jesus said, "As you go..." **Matthew 10:7-8**

I Live Loved radically. **John 15:13** I Live Intentional fearlessly. **1 John 4:18**

I Live Generous joyfully. **2 Corinthians 9:6-7** I Live Hopeful trustfully. **Romans 15:13** I Live Today mindfully. **Colossians 3:1**

With the grace **Acts 4:33**, power **Acts 1:8**, and leading of Holy Spirit **John 16:13**

It's amazing what happens when I align my whole heart **Colossians 3:15-17** - my emotion, my intellect and my action - with the Father's heart. **Matthew 6:8**

Life is short. **James 4:13-17** Forever is real. **1 John 2:17** Loving right matters the most. **1 John 3:16**

Trusting my perfect Father I have perfect peace and perfect love. **1 John 4:7-21**

Choices I make today are gratitude **Philippians 4:6-7**, grace **2 Peter 3:18**, and generosity. **2 Corinthians 8:7**

My life matters to everyone in my everyday world. **Luke 10:5-7**

Little simple gestures change lives daily. **Luke 21:13-15**

Peace rules my heart. **Colossians 3:15**

I CAN change how I feel. **1 Corinthians 6:9-11**

I honour all people. **1 Peter 2:17**

I live above the negativity. **Ephesians 4:29**

The darker the night the brighter my light. **John 8:12**

© Trevor Lund of **RevTrev.com** and founder of Live LIGHT Academy on **LiveLIGHT.ca**

ALSO BY AUTHOR

Find all the current books on **https://livelight.ca/books**

Live LIGHT Gratitude Journal

Live LIGHT Above the Negativity with your Whole Heart

Live LIGHT Gratitude Reflections

Live LIGHT - Judge Right

Live LIGHT - reminded Why your Why matters

Live LIGHT - Get the good God has for you

Live LIGHT - Stop the Worry

Live LIGHT - Tips to fast from Negativity

Live LIGHT - Discover the light and easy yoke of Jesus

Live LIGHT - Overcome habitual sin

Live LIGHT - Examine your heart when life is a mess

Live LIGHT - know how to fast from negativity

Contact the Author on **https://livelight.ca/books** to become a RevTrev Reader and get offers for ARC and sales when they become available.

SCRIPTURE QUOTES

Scripture quotations marked "NIV" taken from the HOLY BIBLE, NEW INTERNATIONAL VERSION®. Copyright © 1973, 1978, 1984, 2011 International Bible Society. Used by permission of Zondervan. All rights reserved

Scripture quotations marked "NLT" taken from the Holy Bible, New Living Translation, copyright 1996. Used by permission of Tyndale House Publishers, Inc., Wheaton, Illinois 60189. All rights reserved.

"Scripture quotations marked "NASB" taken from the New American Standard Bible®,Copyright © 1960, 1962, 1963, 1968, 1971, 1972, 1973,1975, 1977, 1995 by The Lockman Foundation Used by permission." (www.Lockman.org)

"Scripture quotations marked "AMP" or "Amplified" taken from the Amplified® Bible,Copyright © 1954, 1958, 1962, 1964, 1965, 1987 by The Lockman Foundation Used by permission." (www.Lockman.org)

Scripture quotations marked “Phillips” are taken from the New Testament in Modern English, copyright © 1958, 1959, 1960, 1972, J. B. Phillips, and 1947, 1952, 1955, 1957, The Macmillian Company, New York. Used by permission. All rights reserved.

Scripture quotations marked “NJKV” are taken from the New King James Version. Copyright © 1982 by Thomas Nelson Inc. Used by permission. All rights reserved.

Scripture quotations marked “The Message” of “MSG” copyright 1993, 1994, 1995, 1996, 2000, 2001, 2002. Used by permission of NavPress Publishing Group.

Scripture quotations marked Holman Christian Standard Bible (HCSB) Copyright © 1999, 2000, 2002, 2003 by Holman Bible Publishers, Nashville Tennessee. All rights reserved.

www.ingramcontent.com/pod-product-compliance
Lightning Source LLC
Chambersburg PA
CBHW071407090426
42737CB00011B/1383
* 9 7 8 1 8 9 7 4 0 9 2 9 9 *